MARTIN LUTHER KING JR.

Fighting for Civil Rights

MARTIN LUTHER KING JR.

Fighting for Civil Rights

Michael A. Schuman and Anne E. Schraff

Enslow Publishing

101 W. 23rd Street
Suite 240
New York, NY 10011
USA

enslow.com

Published in 2018 by Enslow Publishing, LLC.
101 W. 23rd Street, Suite 240, New York, NY 10011

Library of Congress Cataloging-in-Publication Data

Names: Schuman, Michael, author. | Schraff, Anne E., author.
Title: Martin Luther King Jr. : fighting for civil rights / Michael A. Schuman and
Anne E. Schraff.
Description: New York, NY : Enslow Publishing, [2018] | Series: Rebels with a cause
| Includes bibliographical references and index. | Audience: Grades 7-12.
Identifiers: LCCN 2017003097 | ISBN 9780766085114 (library-bound)
Subjects: LCSH: King, Martin Luther, Jr., 1929-1968--Juvenile literature. | African
Americans—Biography—Juvenile literature. | Civil rights workers—United States—
Biography—Juvenile literature. | Baptists—United States—Clergy—Biography—
Juvenile literature. | African Americans—Civil rights—History—20th century—
Juvenile literature. | Civil rights movements—United States—History—20th
century—Juvenile literature.
Classification: LCC E185.97.K5 S38 2017 | DDC 323.092 [B] —dc23
LC record available at https://lccn.loc.gov/2017003097

Printed in the United States of America

To Our Readers: We have done our best to make sure all website addresses in this
book were active and appropriate when we went to press. However, the author
and the publisher have no control over and assume no liability for the material
available on those websites or on any websites they may link to. Any comments or
suggestions can be sent by email to customerservice@enslow.com.

Photo Credits: Cover, pp. 3, 7, 35, 47, 54, 85, 92–93, 98 Bettmann/Getty Images;
p. 11 LatitudeStock/Alamy Stock Photo; pp. 12–13 Hulton Archive/Archive Photos/
Getty Images; pp. 18–19 Everett Collection Inc/Alamy Stock Photo; p. 25 Dozier
Mobley/Hulton Archive/Getty Images; p. 29 Mondadori Portfolio/Getty Images;
p. 31 Bridgeman Images; p. 36 Underwood Archives/Archive Photos/Getty Images;
p. 43 Keystone Pictures USA/Alamy Stock Photo; pp. 50, 57, 60–61 © AP Images;
pp. 66–67, 74 AFP/Getty Images; pp. 69, 78–79 MPI/Archive Photos/Getty Images;
pp. 76–77 PhotoQuest/Archive Photos/Getty Images; p. 81 Afro Newspaper/Gado/
Archive Photos/Getty Images; pp. 88–89 Miami Herald/Tribune News Service/Getty
Images; p. 97 Raymond Boyd/Michael Ochs Archives/Getty Images; pp. 102–103
Timothy A. Clary/AFP/Getty Images; p. 105 Jewel Samad/AFP/Getty Images; interior
pages borders, pp. 6–7 background Eky Studio/Shutterstock.com.

CONTENTS

INTRODUCTION

Wednesday, September 3, 1958, dawned quietly in Montgomery, Alabama, but it wouldn't be quiet for long. Martin Luther King Jr., then a twenty-nine-year-old minister, tried to enter the Montgomery County Courthouse. He was with two other people. One was his wife, Coretta Scott King. The other was his friend and fellow civil rights activist, Ralph David Abernathy. The Kings were there to support Abernathy, who had been physically attacked in late August. Abernathy was to testify against the assailant. It was well known that separate and unfair laws governed the lives of black and white people in Alabama. A trio of whites would likely have had no trouble entering the courthouse. But that would not be the case for three African Americans.

As they neared the courthouse door, a white guard shouted at King that because he had no business there, he should stay out. King asked if he could speak with a

King is surrounded by supporters as he enters a Montgomery, Alabama, courthouse in September 1958.

friend's lawyer. Two white police officers appeared. "Boy, you done done it," one of the officers yelled at King. "Let's go."[1] Startled, King did not move. One police officer jerked King's arm behind his back and started dragging him away. The officers roughly pulled him down the sidewalk and around the corner to the police station. Coretta King watched in horror as her husband was hauled down the street. As she ran after him, one of the officers turned and snapped, "Gal, you want to go too? Just nod your head."[2]

King cautioned his wife to say nothing. The couple had two small children at home. King was being arrested. If his wife also ended up in jail, there would be nobody to care for the children. So Coretta King remained silent.

King was taken before the desk sergeant at the police station. The sergeant took one look at the young minister and ordered him locked up. King was hustled down a dark corridor to a cell door. He was frisked for weapons. Then one of the officers grabbed King by the throat, choking him before flinging him into the cell and slamming the door.

Martin Luther King Jr., was well known in the United States as a civil rights leader. But the police officers who treated him so roughly did not know who they were dealing with. Nor did they notice the photographer on the street taking pictures of the brutal arrest.

When Montgomery authorities realized they had arrested Martin Luther King Jr., they quickly released him. He was told he would be charged only with failure to obey an officer. That night King told his wife, "I've had enough."[3] He was tired of the way black people were routinely mistreated by the law. He decided not to pay his fine and to go to jail instead as a protest.

When King was tried and convicted, he was fined ten dollars or fourteen days in jail. King declared to the court that he would not pay a fine "for an act that I did not commit and above all for brutal treatment that I did not deserve."[4] Fearing more bad publicity, the officials of Montgomery County paid King's fine.

Martin Luther King Jr., would see the insides of many more jail cells and courtrooms in his struggle to, as he put it that day, "wipe out the scourge of brutality and violence inflicted upon Negroes who seek only to walk with dignity before God and Man."

Life with Mother Dear and Daddy

Martin Luther King Jr. was born in a stately two-and-a-half-story house on Auburn Avenue in Atlanta, Georgia. The date was January 15, 1929, and legal segregation was the rule in the Deep South. African Americans and whites were ordered by law to live in separate neighborhoods.

King's neighborhood was known as Sweet Auburn. It was given that name because it was a rare oasis of opportunity for African Americans. The neighborhood boasted black physicians, dentists, attorneys, and business entrepreneurs. That does not mean that there were no poor people in Sweet Auburn. Mixed in among the proud homes like King's birthplace were the shotgun row houses of the economically disadvantaged. King's neighborhood played a large role in influencing the man he would grow up to be.

King's name at birth was Michael King. It was changed to Martin Luther King Jr. when he was about five. There are different versions of how and why his name was changed. One is that it was a simple error typed on his birth certificate. Another is that Martin's father changed his son's name to pay respect to his father (Martin's grandfather), who had preferred to be called Martin Luther. A third version is that his father was

Martin Luther King Jr.'s birthplace in Atlanta still stands and is open to the public for guided tours.

inspired by the sixteenth century Protestant religious reformer, Martin Luther.

Martin, called M. L. by his family, was born into a strong Baptist tradition. His mother, Alberta Williams King, was the daughter of the Reverend Adam Daniel Williams, pastor of Ebenezer Baptist Church in Atlanta. M. L.'s father was assistant pastor at the same church.

M. L.'s father, the Reverend Mike King, was a strong, tough-minded man. Born on a sharecropping farm in central Georgia, he had spent his youth working the fields with a plow driven by a mule. As a boy, his first chore

Left to right: Mike King, Alberta Williams King, Coretta Scott King, and Christine Farris. They are about to board an airplane to take them to Martin's Nobel Prize presentation in Oslo, Norway.

every morning was to groom the mule, brushing the animal's coat. Teased that he was beginning to smell like a mule, the teenager declared defiantly, "I don't think like a mule."[1]

Mike had a difficult childhood, as his father was an alcoholic. When he was just fifteen, Mike intervened to protect his mother from his father's drunken rages.

Early in his life, Mike saw white people abusing blacks. One day, when he failed to move fast enough to bring water to a white employer, he, too, was struck. Mike worked at many jobs, including helping a mechanic in a repair shop, but he was always fascinated by the emotional preachers at the Baptist pulpit. He felt called to the ministry, so he struggled to pay for the education that would open that door for him. After he earned a college degree in religion, he became a Baptist preacher. M. L.'s mother, Alberta Williams, had grown up with a comfortable life as the daughter of a pastor, and received a good education. In the early 1920s, Mike King began dating Alberta, taking her for drives in his Model T Ford. She was a shy young woman, and Mike had a strong, dynamic personality. The couple married on Thanksgiving Day in 1926. They moved into the upstairs of Alberta's parents' twelve-room house. Mike King became the assistant pastor in his father-in-law's church.

A daughter, Christine, was born to the family, followed a year later by the birth of M. L. The third and last child was Alfred Daniel. The King children enjoyed a happy life in the large house on Auburn Avenue. M. L. called it "a

WHAT IS SHARECROPPING?

When slavery ended, many black men became sharecroppers. Sharecropping is a system in which a landowner rents land to a tenant in return for a percentage of the produce grown on that land. After the Civil War ended in 1865, many freed slaves expected to receive land from the federal government, but they didn't receive any form of aid at all. Thus, the men rented small plots of land, but they had no money for seeds, equipment, or even food. Oftentimes, the interest rate on these loans was very high and the men struggled to get out of debt. Many historians state that this created a new and unfair economic system that was similar to slavery itself.

very congenial home situation," in a family where "love was central."[2]

An Active Childhood

The Kings lived in a pleasant middle-class African American neighborhood. M. L. was an active, athletic boy who enjoyed playing basketball with his friends in the large vacant lot behind his house. He flew kites, made model airplanes, and rode his bicycle through the streets. A favorite indoor activity was sliding down the banister of the two-story Victorian house. Once, when M. L. leaned too hard on the banister, he went flying and bounced through an open door into the cellar. Remarkably, he came out of the fall unhurt.

M. L. later praised his father as "a real father," who "always put his family first."[3] He called him "Daddy," and said he was "as strong in his will as he is in his body."[4] Mike King was muscular, weighing more than 200 pounds (91 kilograms). M. L. called his mother Mother Dear. She was a short, quiet woman who rarely lost her temper. She dressed nicely and had a friendly smile and a warm greeting for everyone.

The relative who held an extra special place in M. L.'s heart was his mother's mother, Grandmother Williams. M. L. later called her a "saintly grandmother."[5] She told the children Bible stories, and M. L. felt that he was her favorite.

In the spring of 1931, Reverend Adam Daniel Williams died, and M. L.'s father became pastor of Ebenezer Baptist Church. He increased church membership and renovated the church building. By the mid-1930s, Mike King was a respected African American leader in Atlanta. He had joined the National Association for the Advancement of Colored People (NAACP), and he was ready to challenge the evils of segregation. He preached about black voters' rights at a time when only whites could vote. In 1935, he led one thousand blacks in a voter registration drive. He also campaigned successfully for equal pay for black teachers.

One day when M. L. was small, he was out with his father when a police officer pulled the car over for driving past a stop sign. The white officer called out, "All right, boy, pull over and let me see your license." M. L.'s father pointed to his son beside him and said, "This is a boy. I'm a man, and until you call me one, I will not listen to you."[6] The officer wrote the ticket and left.

Young M. L. had an incredible memory. By the age of five he could recite entire Bible passages and sing hymns using all the correct words. He was so smart that his parents sent him to school a year early. When M. L. was asked his age, he truthfully said he was five. The school sent him home with instructions to his parents to wait a year before sending him back. The school was not for five year olds.

At age six, M. L. started singing in church groups, accompanied by his mother on the piano. He was an instant celebrity, performing emotional gospel songs with great fervor. He often sang "I Want to Be More and More Like Jesus."[7] To see the small boy expressing such sincere faith caused some of the congregation to weep and cry out in joy.

M. L.'s father had grown up in grim poverty, and he wanted better lives for his own children. He prayed daily that his children would have an easier time than he had. Mike King was very strict with money, and he ran the house with firm rules. The children always got what they needed, but for extras like ice cream and sodas, they had to spend their allowances. In the King house there was one authority: Daddy King. Neither his wife nor his mother-in-law, Grandma Williams, ever questioned that fact. When M. L. or his sister or brother misbehaved, there was surely a punishment. The children did not dare act rude or sassy lest their father strap them. Sometimes he made the children whip each other for misdeeds. Most of all, M. L. hated to disappoint his father. Letting his father down hurt M. L. more than the whipping that would surely follow.

One time when Alfred Daniel, known as A. D., was teasing his sister, Christine, M. L. became so upset that he hit his brother with the telephone. Alfred was knocked out by the impact. Daddy King punished M. L. for this act of violence, whipping him until tears flowed from the boy's eyes. Even so, M. L. did not object. He took the punishment in silence. Grandma Williams, however, was so distraught to see him whipped so hard that she rushed from the room crying. But she did not try to stop his father from punishing the boy.

M. L. knew that whenever he was punished, it hurt his grandmother, and that fact made him love her dearly. One day when the boys were playing, A. D. slid down the banister and accidentally kicked Grandma Williams, who was standing at the bottom of the stairs. The elderly lady fell to the floor and did not move. M. L. ran to his grandmother and stared down at her in fear. He thought she had been killed by the accident. He felt guilty that his reckless play with his brother had caused the death of his beloved grandmother. M. L. was so guilt-ridden and heartbroken that he ran up to his room and threw himself from the open window, dropping two stories to the earth below. M. L. lay there as his relatives, including Grandma Williams, now up and feeling fine, hurried to his side. When M. L. heard his grandmother's voice calling to him, he got to his feet, unhurt.

M. L's best friend in early childhood was a white boy whose father owned a store across the street. In September 1935, the two six year olds started school. M. L. went to the school for black children, and his friend went to the whites-only school. M. L. expected that they would still get together after school, and he was deeply hurt when the white boy said their friendship was over. The boy's mother would not let them play anymore.

A Friendship Ends

Traditionally at that time in the South, white and black children could be close friends when they were very young, but as they came of school age the relationships had to end. In later years, M. L.

Legal segregation in the US South was the rule for decades. In this photo, a young boy stands by a segregated water fountain in North Carolina.

would recall the loss of his friend as one of the most painful experiences of his childhood. "I never will forget what a great shock this was to me," he said.[8] M. L. was so troubled that he struggled with feelings of hatred toward white people. When he talked to his parents about it, they told him it was his Christian duty to love everyone, no matter the color of their skin. The boy asked himself, "How could I love a race of people who hated me and who had been responsible for breaking me up with one of my best childhood friends?"[9]

On the heels of losing his friend, M. L. went downtown with his father for a new pair of shoes. When Daddy King sat down to help his son try on some shoes, a white clerk hurried over to tell them to go to the rear of the store. African Americans were not allowed to shop in the main part of the store, he said. M. L.'s father angrily left without buying anything.

M. L. soon became aware of all the restrictions on African Americans. They could not use the public parks or eat inside the restaurants. They were welcome at just one theater, where the movies were all years old. At age eight, when M. L. accidentally stepped on a white woman's foot, she slapped him across the face and insulted him. One day, after seeing a brutal attack on a black passenger, M. L.'s father refused to ride the segregated city buses anymore. Daddy King said, "I don't care how long I have to live with this system, I will never accept it."[10]

On May 18, 1941, twelve-year-old M. L. sneaked out to watch a parade without his parents' permission. He was enjoying the colorful marching bands when someone he knew rushed up to tell him that something terrible had happened to Grandmother Williams at home. M. L. had thought she was at church, and he ran home, his heart pounding with fear. There, he learned that his grandmother had suffered a heart attack and died on the way to the hospital.

Once more, M. L. was stricken with sorrow and guilt. He asked himself why God had allowed such a thing to happen. Why had God taken his grandmother, the person he loved most in the world? In his tortured mind, M. L. believed that God was punishing him for his disobedience in going to the parade without his parents' knowledge.

The boy could not bear the torment he felt. He rushed up to his room and once again hurled himself through the open window. His body smacked the ground below. As he lay bruised and trembling, his parents rushed to his side. He was not seriously hurt, but for many days he stayed in his room, crying. M. L.'s father tried to soothe him, explaining that God took people whenever He was ready for them, and it had nothing to do with anything M. L. had done.

Growing up in a deeply religious family, M. L. had always believed that when good people die they go to heaven, where they are reunited with their loved ones. The death of his grandmother affected him so profoundly that from that day on, his belief in life after death was unshakable.

> **Years later, referring to his grandmother's death, King said, "This is why today I am such a strong believer in personal immortality."[11]**

Not long after the death of Grandma Williams, the King family moved to a two-story brick house in a better neighborhood. The children were growing into their teens. Christine was very obedient, A. D. was sometimes rebellious, and M. L. could be obedient at times and rebellious at others. He continued to get whippings from his father until he was fifteen years old.

As a teenager, M. L. out-wrestled his friends, played the piano, and enjoyed opera. He was a student at Booker T. Washington High School, and learning came easily to him. He loved to read and was always in the middle of a book. He also enjoyed eating soul food, especially fried chicken, corn bread, collard greens, ham hocks, and bacon drippings. M. L. struggled with conflicting feelings about his father. He loved and respected his father, but he wanted to be independent, too. He felt certain that he never wanted to follow in his father's footsteps and become a minister.

In the eleventh grade, M. L. entered an oratorical contest. His topic was "The Negro and the Constitution." M. L. won a prize for his speech, and he was in high spirits riding home on the bus from Dublin, Georgia, to Atlanta. At a stop along the way, some white passengers boarded the bus. There were not enough empty seats, so the white driver ordered the black students to get up and give their seats to the white newcomers. M. L. wanted to defy the order, but his teacher, Mrs. Bradley, whom he respected, persuaded him to move. For the next 90 miles (145 kilometers) to Atlanta, M. L. and the other black students had to stand in the aisle. King later said, "It was the angriest I have ever been in my life."[12]

In the spring of 1944, fifteen year-old M. L. passed a special examination for early admittance to Atlanta's Morehouse College. That summer, Morehouse sponsored him for a job at a tobacco farm in Connecticut. M. L. had delivered newspapers since age eleven, but this would be his first real job. The fact that it was many miles from home appealed to the restless teenager. He was getting away for the first time in his life.

Even though the job entailed long hours working with tobacco plants in the hot sun, M. L. enjoyed it very much. On weekends he went into the nearby city of Hartford, where he had his first taste of integration. He spoke of an "exhilarating sense of freedom."[13] In a June 1944 letter to his father, he wrote, "The white people here are very nice. We go to any place we want to and sit anywhere we want to."[14]

Young Martin Luther King Jr. was getting his first glimpse of an integrated world. He would later devote his life to trying to make this a reality all over America.

When Martin Met Coretta

Even though King had finished only his junior year of high school in June 1944, he was admitted into college in September that year. Because many African American males were fighting overseas in World War II, there was a shortage of male students in traditionally African American universities and colleges such as Morehouse College. These colleges decided that a way to make up for this shortage of male students was to admit intelligent and capable high school juniors. Because Martin was only fifteen, he had not given much thought to a career. At times he thought he might make a good doctor or lawyer.

King finally chose sociology as his major and English as his minor. To his distress, he discovered that his schooling had not prepared him well for college-level work. He was reading at just an eighth-grade level, and the teachers at Morehouse demanded much more than that. It became painfully clear to King that the black schools he had attended in Atlanta were not good enough. They did not fully prepare their students to succeed in college. King's English teacher at Morehouse gave him a C-plus, but commented that "he would have had an A based just on interest."[1]

Martin Luther King Jr. preaches from the pulpit at the Ebenezer Baptist Church around 1960.

King's professors at Morehouse described modern clergymen as rational beings, who were spiritually and intellectually strong, and determined to help make people's lives better. This depiction appealed to King, and he opened his mind to the possibility of entering the ministry. At the age of seventeen, he made the decision to become a Baptist minister. He said later of that moment, "I came to see that God had placed a responsibility upon my shoulders."[2]

When King told his father of his decision, the senior King was delighted but did not reveal this to his son. Instead, he suggested that the young man preach a trial

MOREHOUSE COLLEGE

Morehouse College has a long and storied history. It is an all-male college founded in Augusta, Georgia, just two years after the Civil War ended. In 1879, the college was relocated to Atlanta. By the 1920s, it had become a widely respected African American college. Martin Luther King Jr. is the college's best-known alumnus, but he is hardly the only famous one. Other notable alumni include: filmmaker Spike Lee; businessman Herman Cain; actor Samuel L. Jackson; former US Attorney General David Satcher; and Olympic track star and gold medalist Edwin Moses.

sermon in one of the smaller auditoriums in Ebenezer Baptist Church. When Martin Luther King Jr. began preaching, his sermon drew so many people that they had to move the service to the main auditorium. Daddy King felt grateful to have such a son.

In 1947, eighteen-year-old Martin Luther King Jr. was appointed assistant pastor of Ebenezer Baptist Church. In the summers he worked as a laborer on the railroad, loading and unloading trains in Atlanta's suffocating heat. There, he was among a class of black people he had never met before—the hardworking black poor. For King, it was a glimpse into another world.

In the spring of 1948, King graduated from Morehouse College with a degree in sociology. He decided to pursue his divinity degree at Crozer Theological Seminary. King longed to be his own man, and the college in Chester, Pennsylvania, on the banks of the Delaware River, seemed an ideal place for stepping outside his father's large shadow.

Crozer Seminary had one hundred students, including twelve women and six blacks. For the first time in his life, King was in a mostly white school, competing with the brightest students. He received As in all his subjects. His time at Morehouse College had erased the gap in his education from Atlanta's segregated school system.

The Strategy of Nonviolence

It was at Crozer that Martin Luther King Jr., began seriously studying nonviolence as a philosophy. At first he believed that war could be a "negative good in stopping the spread of an evil."[3] Then he attended a lecture given by Mordecai Johnson, president of Howard University, in

Washington, DC, on the life of Mohandas K. Gandhi of India. King later described being "electrified" by Gandhi's philosophy.[4] He read six books on Gandhi's life and embraced the idea that love had the power to overcome all evil. King now believed that doing nothing in the face of evil was cowardly, but confronting it nonviolently was the height of courage. He decided to live by the principle that nonviolent action would lead to "the creation of the beloved community," while the "aftermath of violence is tragic bitterness."[5]

In June 1951, King was awarded a degree in divinity, graduating at the top of his class. He also received a $1,300 scholarship for graduate school. He decided to attend Boston University's prestigious School of Theology, where he would pursue his PhD—the highest university degree—in systematic theology.

After a summer in Atlanta, King drove to Boston in his brand-new green Chevrolet, a gift from his father. He had a problem finding a place to live in the city. He went to many places that advertised rooms for rent—but "they were for rent until they found out I was a Negro, and suddenly they had just been rented," he said.[6] Eventually, he did find a room.

King joined the lively social life of Boston, frequenting the Western Lunch Box, which served the kind of southern food he was used to. At night, he and his friends enjoyed hot jazz at the Totem Pole. Though he dated many young women, King could not find that one special person he might want to settle down with. One day, while having lunch with a married friend, Mary Powell, a student at the New England Conservatory of Music in Boston, King asked, "Do you know any nice, attractive young ladies?"[7]

Powell mentioned Coretta Scott, a fellow student at the conservatory, whom she described as "pretty and

This is a picture of a covered market in Boston, as the city looked when the Kings lived there in the 1950s.

intelligent."[8] King called Scott at home, introducing himself as a friend of Mary Powell's. He said he had heard "wonderful things" about her. Could he take her to lunch? Scott agreed to the lunch date, and King promised to pick her up at the conservatory in his car. He told her the trip usually took ten minutes, but he was so eager to meet her, he would make it in seven.

Scott and King lunched in a cafeteria with cold rain pouring down outside. Later, Scott recalled her first impressions of King. "How short he seems, how unimpressive," she thought.[9] But as King talked, Scott found that "he radiated so much charm" that he became "much better looking."[10] As for King, his first impression of Coretta Scott was very favorable. He liked her hair, her shy, pretty smile, and her personality. They talked for a long time, and as King was driving Scott back to the conservatory, he said, "Do you know what? You have everything I have ever wanted in a wife." He then named all of her qualities that attracted him: "character, intelligence, personality, and beauty."[11] Scott was astonished by the comment, but agreed to let him call her again.

Martin Luther King Jr. was taken with Coretta Scott from the first night he saw her. Not so for Coretta, who took several more dates to fall in love.

Different Backgrounds

Coretta Scott's economic background was much different than King's. She was born on a farm in rural Marion, Alabama. Over the years, her hardworking parents had managed to create a comfortable life for their family. Scott gained an education through scholarships, graduating from Antioch College in 1951 with a degree in music and education. She had a lovely mezzo-soprano voice. She hoped for a musical career and was in no rush to get married. She also had a distaste for Baptist preachers, believing them to be narrow-minded, overly pious people.

At a party they both attended in suburban Watertown, Massachusetts, Coretta Scott noticed that other women were attracted to Martin. This impressed her, and she accepted more dates with him. The young couple walked together along the ocean and went to concerts in

Martin Luther King Jr. and Coretta Scott smile at their wedding in 1953.

Boston's Symphony Hall. They ice-skated and shared their philosophies of life. King told Scott that he wanted to help humanity. He also frankly admitted that he saw the role of a wife as homemaker and mother. Scott realized that any dreams of a musical career would end if she married King.

As their relationship grew more serious, King introduced Scott to his family. After some initial stress, Daddy King approved the union. In June 1953, twenty-four-year-old Martin Luther King Jr. and his family, traveling in a motorcade, pulled up at the Scott home in Marion, Alabama. The Scotts all liked King, and on June 18, Daddy King performed the marriage ceremony for the couple on the lawn. King's younger brother, A. D., was best man.

Because none of the local hotels would accommodate African Americans, Coretta and Martin spent their wedding night at the home of a friend, who was a funeral director. "Do you know," King later joked, "we spent our honeymoon at a funeral parlor?"[12]

Back in Boston, the newlyweds rented a four-room apartment and resumed their studies. In June 1954, Coretta Scott King would graduate from the conservatory. While she was busy studying, King was a real help at home. He cleaned the apartment, washed the clothes, and hung them to dry in the kitchen. He cooked, too, often preparing his favorite dish—cabbage, pork chops, and pigs' feet.

Like his father, King was very thrifty. He kept a three-ring notebook in which he listed all family expenses. He recorded every purchase, no matter how small. In the summer of 1953, he was working on his doctoral thesis, along with doing the housework. A thesis is a long, detailed research paper required to earn a PhD. The young couple was short of money, and King knew he needed to find employment as a minister soon.

King soon received an offer to become pastor of Dexter Avenue Baptist Church in Montgomery, Alabama. This was the church attended by many black professors at Alabama State University, as well as other black professionals. King flew there in January 1954 to deliver a trial sermon. It would give the congregation an opportunity to see if the prospective minister would fit in. The congregation loved the young minister and his sermon. King was offered the job at $4,300 a year, the highest salary paid to a black minister in Montgomery.

When King told his wife about his warm reception in Alabama, she had mixed feelings. She, like her husband, enjoyed the integrated atmosphere of Boston. She recalled the harsh segregation of her youth, and she dreaded returning to the South. Complicating the decision was Daddy King's offer for his son to become associate pastor at Ebenezer Baptist Church in Atlanta.

Martin Luther King Jr. urged his wife to take a look at Dexter Avenue Baptist Church before they made their decision. In Alabama, Coretta King was depressed to see black people riding in the backs of buses and the general oppression of the black community. She shuddered at the thought of bringing up their children in that atmosphere. But she told her husband, "If this is what you want, I'll make myself happy in Montgomery."[13]

The Bus Was Empty!

The years 1954 and 1955 proved to be busy times for the Kings. They moved to Montgomery, but Martin hadn't finished working on his PhD at Boston University. So he spent much of that year and a half travelling up to Boston to complete his school-work, and back to Montgomery to preach. After finally receiving his PhD in June 1955, Martin moved permanently to Montgomery to be with Coretta. King was enthusiastic about his job. He put hours into writing and memorizing sermons. He also managed to find the time to do other duties required of a minister, such as visiting the sick.

On November 17, 1955, the Kings celebrated the birth of their first child, Yolanda Denise, nicknamed Yoki. King said that she "was a big little girl—she weighed nine pounds and eleven ounces. She kept her father quite busy walking the floor."[1]

In the mid-1950s, Montgomery, like most Southern cities, was strictly segregated. In 1954, the Supreme Court had ruled in *Brown v. Board of Education of Topeka, Kansas*, that having separate schools for blacks and whites was unconstitutional. This gave African Americans hope that the walls of segregation were beginning to crumble.

Segregated buses were a way of life in Montgomery, Alabama, in 1955.

One sore point in Montgomery was the bus system. The majority of riders were black, but seating on the city buses was segregated with black people forced to sit in the back. They were often treated rudely by drivers.

On December 1, 1955, Rosa Parks, a black seamstress and NAACP secretary, was taking her usual ride home after a long day at work. The seats in the white section of the bus were filled, and more white passengers boarded the bus. The driver walked down the aisle and told Parks and some other black riders to yield their seats to the white passengers who had just arrived. Parks politely refused. As a result, the police were called and Parks was taken to jail.

Rosa Parks gets fingerprinted following her arrest for refusing to give up her seat to a white passenger.

By refusing to move to the back of a segregated bus in Montgomery, Alabama, in 1955, activist Rosa Parks energized the Civil Rights movement.

The arrest of the soft-spoken, well-respected Rosa Parks energized the civil rights movement in Montgomery. King and an outspoken young black minister named Ralph Abernathy attended a meeting of religious leaders to discuss what to do. They decided to boycott the Montgomery bus system and demand that its twenty thousand black riders be treated more fairly. A one-day bus boycott was planned for December 5, the same day Rosa Parks was scheduled to be tried for refusing to give up her seat.

Would They Not Ride the Buses?

On the morning of the boycott, there was great tension in the black community. The Kings waited anxiously to see if the African Americans of Montgomery would unite to avoid riding the buses. Many would have to walk long distances or find rides with the lucky few who owned cars. The winter weather was chilly and often rainy. King was not sure that so many weary, working people would be ready to make the sacrifice.

At 6 a.m. Coretta King, who had been watching from the front window of their home, cried, "Martin! Martin! Come quickly." King joined his wife at the window to see the first bus of the South Jackson line rolling by. Pointing to the bus, Coretta King said, "Darling, it's empty!"[2] The Kings counted eight black passengers all morning on buses that were usually packed with black riders. It was the same for the rest of the day. The boycott was a huge success.

Rosa Parks went to court and was convicted of violating the Alabama desegregation law. She was ordered to pay a fine of ten dollars, plus four dollars in court costs. That was exactly what the civil rights leaders had hoped would happen. Now they could challenge Parks's conviction in the courts and try to use the legal system to overturn bus segregation as unconstitutional.

A group of Montgomery ministers formed the Montgomery Improvement Association (MIA) and King was elected president. The boycott continued past the first day, and the MIA made its mission known. It demanded that black bus drivers be hired for routes that were mostly black; that seating be handled on a first come, first served basis; and that black passengers be treated with courtesy. As leader of the MIA, King spoke eloquently to his followers, telling them to "protest courageously, and yet with dignity and Christian love."[3] The congregation greeted King's call with thunderous applause. For months to come, 95 percent of the black riders of Montgomery boycotted the buses. Volunteers were organized by the MIA to answer phones and coordinate rides with a fleet of 150 private cars, carpools, and black taxis, which lowered their rates. [4] The volunteers ran a public and private transportation system. King later said that he was so busy he hardly had "time to breathe."[5]

A hectic schedule was not the only price King paid for leading the boycott. He was harassed and threatened. He was arrested in Montgomery for driving 30 miles per hour (48 kilometers per hour) in a 25 mile-per-hour (50 kilometer-per-hour) zone, and he was placed in a jail cell with drunks and serious criminals. When hundreds of angry African Americans surrounded the jail, King was released with the promise that he would appear for his trial.

Threats and Hate Mail

Threats and hate mail arrived daily at the parsonage. King worried that something would happen to him and that his followers would react with violence. He pleaded with them never to respond to violence with more violence. He also worried deeply about the safety of his wife and baby daughter. Looking at his wife and sleeping child, he thought, "They can be taken away from me at any moment."[6]

One night, the pressures were building up, and King felt he could not endure them any more. He bent over the kitchen table and prayed for strength. He felt as if a voice said to him, "Stand up for righteousness, stand up for justice, stand up for truth; and God will be at your side forever." King said of that moment, "I experienced the presence of the Divine as I had never experienced Him before."[7]

On Monday night, January 30, 1956, King's worst fears nearly came true. He was at a meeting when someone rushed up to him with frightening news. A bomb had exploded at his home with his wife and daughter inside. King rushed home to find that Coretta's foresight had kept them unhurt. Hearing a thud on the front porch, she ran with the baby toward the rear of the house to escape the blast she expected would follow. She was right: several sticks of dynamite exploded, and the glass from the front window shattered into the house.

Thousands of outraged African Americans gathered at the bombed King home, demanding retaliation. King addressed them, saying, "We must love our white brothers no matter what they do to us."[8] King's powers of persuasion were so effective that violence was averted and the crowd ended up singing the hymn "Amazing Grace."

Frustrated by the economic losses to the city bus system and to downtown stores, the Montgomery County Grand Jury indicted King and 118 other civil rights leaders on charges of running an illegal boycott. King was quickly convicted and immediately filed for an appeal. The fates of the others were left suspended until King's appeal was decided. King's appeal was heard on June 4, 1956, by a three-judge panel in federal court. They held that bus segregation was unconstitutional. Not long after, the Supreme Court affirmed the decision.

King called the end of bus segregation a "glorious daybreak at the end of a long night."[9] Some angry whites responded to the decision with threats and violence, but for the most part the desegregation of the buses went smoothly. On December 20, 1956, King himself boarded a bus in Montgomery, and the white driver said cordially, "I believe you are Reverend King, aren't you?" When King said he was, the driver said, "We are glad to have you this morning."[10]

A New Spotlight

The successful Montgomery bus boycott thrust the twenty-seven-year-old King into the spotlight not only in the United States but around the world. Many news agencies from foreign countries had been observing the 381-day boycott, marveling at the thousands of adults and schoolchildren who walked to avoid riding segregated buses.

The next two years were filled with dramatic events in the lives of the King family. On February 18, 1957, *Time* magazine featured a lengthy cover story on King, describing him as a "scholarly Negro Baptist minister who in little more than a year has risen from nowhere to become one of the nation's remarkable leaders of men."[11]

In March 1957, Martin and Coretta King took a trip to Africa to celebrate the country of Ghana's independence from colonial rule. It was their first long vacation since their marriage, and it was an awesome experience for the young southern couple. Fifty thousand Ghanaians, many in tribal dress, rejoiced as the British flag was lowered and the new red, green, and yellow flag of independent Ghana was raised. King commented that "both segregation in America and colonialism in Africa were based on the same thing—white supremacy and contempt for life."[12]

Later that year, King called 115 black leaders to Montgomery to discuss strategies for advancing civil rights in the United States. They formed the Southern Christian Leadership Conference (SCLC) and chose King as their president. The goal of the SCLC was to become involved in black churches all over the South to support and coordinate civil rights activities. The first project was to be a drive to register as many new black voters as possible.

In October 1957, Coretta and Martin King welcomed a son, Martin Luther King, III. "Little Marty" cried so loudly that his dad said he would probably be a preacher when he grew up. Also in 1957, Martin Luther King Jr. received the NAACP's highest honor, the Spingarn Medal, in recognition of his work on behalf of African Americans.

The next year, he traveled north on a tour with his first book, *Stride Toward Freedom: The Montgomery Story.*

On September 19, King was signing books at Blumstein's Department Store in Harlem, a mostly black section of New York City. A black woman, Izola Curry, approached him and cried out, "Luther King, I've been after you for five years."[13] Then she lunged at King, driving a long, razor-sharp letter opener deep into his chest. King was taken to a Harlem hospital, where an interracial team of doctors led by Dr. Aubre D. Maynard fought to save his life. The letter-opener blade was so close to King's aorta—the body's largest artery—that if he had sneezed he would have died of a massive hemorrhage. The operation to remove the blade took three hours, and the incision in King's chest was made in the shape of a cross. Maynard commented, "He is a minister. It seemed appropriate."[14]

Izola Curry was sent to a mental hospital for the criminally insane. Speaking of her later, King said, "Get her healed."[15] Pneumonia slowed King's recovery, but he was released from the hospital on October 3, and he spent the next three weeks recuperating at a friend's house.

The following year, 1959, the Kings had an opportunity to visit India. King had looked forward to visiting the birthplace of the man whose philosophy had so shaped his thinking: Mahatma Gandhi. When he and Coretta arrived in India in February, King said he came "as a pilgrim."[16] The Kings toured the country, taking long train rides to visit multiple cities. They were touched by the poverty and the patience of so many people. King said he had found a place for America to store all the surplus food we had—"in the wrinkled stomachs of starving people in Asia and Africa."[17] He spent a day at the spot where Gandhi started a 218-mile (351-km) walk

Martin and Coretta Scott King lay a wreath at a memorial for Mahatma Gandhi on a 1959 visit to New Delhi, India.

to protest injustice. King was moved by Gandhi's success in using love, goodwill, and a refusal to cooperate with evil to change his world.

After India, the Kings traveled to Jerusalem, Cairo, and Athens. From his time in all these places, King felt a deeper spirituality. He resolved to sleep only four hours a night so that he could devote more time to the civil rights struggle. He also planned to set aside one day a week for fasting and meditation. With his busy schedule, he never accomplished that goal.

WHO WAS "MAHATMA" GANDHI?

Mohandas Gandhi was India's greatest spiritual and political leader. He was a beloved figure among his fellow Indians and was lovingly known as Mahatma, which means "Great Soul." For more than forty years, he used fasting, peaceful resistance, and boycotts to lead the people of India to freedom from British rule. He frequently used nonviolent demonstrations to fight unjust laws and the unfair treatment of certain groups in India. He was assassinated in 1948, the year after he negotiated independence for his country.

In November 1959, King was asked to become co-pastor of Ebenezer Baptist Church in Atlanta with his father. The SCLC was requesting more of King's time for their work, and he could not do all that and be a full-time pastor, too. King made the decision to resign from Dexter Avenue Baptist Church and return to Atlanta. In his farewell sermon to the people at Dexter, he said, "History has thrust upon me a responsibility from which I cannot turn away."[18] He and the congregation ended the service with a tearful rendition of the old hymn "Blest Be the Tie That Binds."

Within one month of Martin Luther King Jr.'s return to Atlanta, he received word that the Montgomery Grand Jury had indicted him for tax fraud. A stunned King was crushed by this attack on his honesty and integrity.

The Jury Chose the "Path of Justice"

K ing was charged by the state of Alabama with two counts of perjury. Perjury means lying under oath in a legal investigation. The charges stated that King did not include his full income when he paid state income tax in 1956 and 1958. They said that King used money from the Montgomery Improvement Association and the Southern Christian Leadership Conference not for activist purposes but for his own use. But King was hardly wealthy. He said, "I own just one piece of property, a 1954 Pontiac ... I am renting the house I live in."[1]

King even lacked the money for a decent legal defense. His friends set up an emergency legal fund to help him. Nobel Prize–winning diplomat Ralph Bunche believed that most people would know that King was innocent because, "It's the word of the state of Alabama against the word of Martin Luther King. There is no question in my mind which the country will accept."[2] King himself had no such confidence. He lamented that "many people will think I am guilty." He was sure he would be convicted when he went to trial and, he said, "People will believe that I took money that didn't belong to me."[3]

King fell into a deep depression. His enemies had tried firebombing his house, arresting him on false charges, and harassing him with death threats. Now they were

King holds his son Martin Luther King III as he stands by a burnt cross at his Atlanta home in February 1960. The Ku Klux Klan often burned crosses to threaten minorities.

cutting to the heart of King's character. He feared that the charges would destroy his effectiveness in the civil rights struggle. For a while he did not want to face anybody, and he canceled some speeches. But then he decided he had to stand up to this false accusation and get on with his work.

King traveled to Montgomery, Alabama, to join hands with college students who were protesting segregated lunch counters. It was his message to the outside world that he would not be intimidated, even by the income tax evasion accusation.

In May 1960, King met with his legal team. They had already spent ten thousand dollars preparing his defense. King was very upset, saying it was "immoral and impractical" to waste so much money on a defense that was bound to fail.[4] Though certain of his conviction in the Alabama courts, King pinned his hopes on an appeal to the federal courts. His lawyers, on the other hand, kept assuring him that the case against him was so ridiculous that not even a white jury in Alabama would believe it.

On Trial

On Monday, May 23, 1960, King stood trial. His attorneys argued that the whole case was a frame-up. When the prosecution presented its case, the star witness admitted that King was an honest man. Still, King looked at those twelve white men sitting in the jury box, and he thought he knew what was coming—a conviction. The jury deliberated, and on Saturday they gave their verdict: not guilty. King was astonished. He said he had learned a great lesson: "What started out as a bigoted, prejudiced jury" had chosen "the path of justice."[5] With the tax case out of the way, King returned his attention to the sit-ins at segregated lunch counters in the South.

In Atlanta, King met with seventy-five students who were sitting in at the lunch counter at Rich's Department Store. Dick Rich, the owner, cried when he saw King with the demonstrators because he knew the pressure and publicity would mount quickly. King and the students were arrested, and King refused to pay the five-hundred-dollar bond that would release him from jail until his case came before the judge. He insisted he would stay in jail "ten years if necessary."[6] Officials in Atlanta, not wanting bad publicity, dropped all charges against King. But the harassment did not stop. The traffic court judge from neighboring De Kalb County ordered that King be held on another charge. Earlier, King had been cited for driving without a valid license. His Alabama license had expired and he did not yet have a Georgia license. For that offense he had been charged twenty-five dollars and was placed on probation for a year. If he were arrested again during the year for any offense, he would be subject to prison. The arrest at Rich's Department Store was deemed a violation of King's probation.

King was sentenced to four months of hard labor for the probation violation. His supporters were shocked by this turn of events. For King to be ordered to Reidsville Prison for violating probation on a minor traffic offense was unheard of. Coretta King, five months pregnant with their third child, wept in the courtroom. It was the first time she ever cried in public during all the civil rights struggles. When his wife visited him in jail before he was transferred to Reidsville, King told her to "be strong" for him.[7]

This was a typical cell in Reidsville Prison in Georgia.

> **"Cockroaches darted across the cell walls. It was bitter cold. The next day, the guards brought lunch, black-eyed peas and greens, which tasted so bad King could not eat it."**

In the middle of that night, several men came to King's cell shouting for him to get up. A flashlight beam was thrown in his face. King knew all too well that black prisoners roused from jail at night sometimes disappeared. He was not sure what was happening as handcuffs were snapped on his wrists and chains clamped to his legs. The handcuffs were so tight that they bit into his flesh as he was hauled out to a sheriff's car.

After a 300-mile (483-km) drive, King saw the sign for Reidsville Prison looming in the darkness. He was hustled inside and given a prison uniform, white with green stripes down the pant legs. He was placed in the kind of cell reserved for hardened criminals. Cockroaches darted across the cell walls. It was bitter cold. The next day, the guards brought lunch, black-eyed peas and greens, which tasted so bad King could not eat it. He fell ill with a cold and lay feverish on his bunk, wondering what was happening.

Unknown to King, events on the outside were moving swiftly. Massachusetts senator John F. Kennedy, the Democratic candidate for president in the 1960 election, heard of King's plight and called Coretta King to express his concern. Then he called the judge who had sentenced King and demanded to know why bail had not been granted in this case. The judge changed his ruling, and King was immediately released on bail. Word of Kennedy's intervention swept through the black community.

The presidential election was held two weeks later, and Kennedy won with a large majority of black voters. It was a close election, and their votes made a difference.

On January 30, 1961, the Kings' third child, Dexter Scott, was born. King had high hopes for the newly inaugurated John F. Kennedy. He saw in the young president a real chance to have the federal government energetically on the side of the civil rights struggle. But after meeting with Kennedy and his brother, Attorney General Robert Kennedy, King was dissatisfied. The meetings were cordial, but King did not feel that President Kennedy saw ending segregation as a major priority in his administration. Still, as time went by, King hoped the president would become an important ally for civil rights.

In the spring of 1961, the Congress of Racial Equality (CORE), a civil rights group trying to end segregation, sent a large number of young people called freedom riders to challenge the segregation laws in interstate travel. The freedom riders, who were black and white, left Washington aboard Greyhound buses. When they reached Alabama, they were attacked by mobs wielding sticks, brass knuckles, and lead pipes. In one instance, a mob surrounded a bus filled with freedom riders and set it on fire. King saw television coverage of the violent events and flew at once to Montgomery.

At a mass rally at Reverend Ralph Abernathy's church, King spoke while ten thousand angry white people milled outside, shouting and threatening to storm the building. King called Robert Kennedy, who called Alabama governor John Malcolm Patterson and asked for protection for the blacks in the church. Patterson declared martial law: the government would call in the military to keep order. National Guardsmen moved to disperse the white mob. As a result of this and other demonstrations, the Interstate Commerce Commission outlawed segregation on all forms of public transportation.

Disturbing Events in Albany, Georgia

In Albany, Georgia, the Student Nonviolent Coordinating Committee (SNCC, pronounced "snick") was mounting a protest against segregation on buses and trains. In spite of the federal government's desegregation orders, buses and trains continued to be segregated. SNCC held a freedom march in Albany, and five hundred young people were jailed. Many could not afford bail, so they remained behind bars.

Dr. William Anderson, a black physician, called on Martin Luther King Jr. to come down to help what was called the Albany Movement. King arrived on December 15, 1961, with the intention of only making a speech to energize the movement. But he changed his mind and stayed to join in the march. On December 16, King and many others were arrested, charged with parading without a permit. King vowed to spend Christmas in jail to illustrate his commitment to the movement. But city officials bailed him out to prevent the story from making major national news.

When King arrived in Albany, he thought the African American leadership was united, as it had been in Montgomery during the successful bus boycott. Unfortunately it was seriously divided. SNCC was in charge, and the NAACP was not supportive. There was rivalry and jealousy among black leaders.

The black people of Albany loved King, but the leadership was suspicious of him. One black leader said

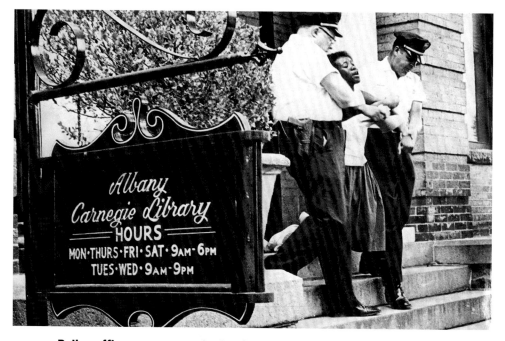

Police officers carry a protestor down the stairs of the Albany, Georgia, Carnegie Library during a civil rights rally.

the Albany Movement needed no "outside help," rejecting King's aid.[8] Although the Albany Movement was an ambitious effort to attack segregation on many fronts, the disunity caused it to fail.

King returned to Atlanta and began work on his second book, *Strength to Love*, in early 1963. During the previous seven years, King had spent more than 75 percent of his time away from home, taking part in civil rights struggles throughout the South. He tried to make the most of what little time he had with his family. On March 28, 1963, the Kings' fourth child, Bernice Albertine, was born.

A few days later, King turned his attention to Birmingham, Alabama. He had two goals for Birmingham:

FATHER MARTIN LUTHER KING JR.

Although Martin Luther King Jr. was a busy man, when he was at home he was a dedicated family man, too. "We had quality time [together]," daughter Yoki later recalled. "Whenever he was home it was as if we were the whole world."[9] King enjoyed lifting the children to the top of the refrigerator and then having them jump into his arms. As the children grew older, they would jump to him from the stairway banister. He never missed a catch.

the first was to force white leaders to begin desegregation. African Americans would apply pressure by boycotting downtown department stores. King's second goal was to draw federal attention to injustices against black people. He planned to use large protest demonstrations to get this message across.

Black leaders were united in Birmingham, but they faced a brutal opponent in the person of Theophilus Eugene "Bull" Connor, Commissioner of Public Safety and supervisor of the police and fire departments. Connor was known both for extreme racism and for using harsh tactics to crush opposition. King anticipated drawing nationwide attention to Birmingham when Connor's troops confronted the demonstrators. King counted on Connor's bullying tactics to rouse mass public sympathy for the cause of civil rights.

5
Up Against Bull Connor

Birmingham is a big city with a thriving steel industry. In the early 1960s, it was also an extremely segregated city. Roughly 40 percent of Birmingham's population was African American.[1] The city also had a sizable amount of Ku Klux Klan (KKK) members. The KKK is an organization that preaches white Christian supremacy. At the time, the KKK regularly committed violent acts against minorities, especially African Americans. They were responsible for dynamite bombings of African American churches and homes of civil rights activists. These happened so often in Birmingham that some called the city "Bombingham."[2] On April 12, 1963, King led a protest march in the city. They had gone only a few blocks when Bull Connor ordered the police to arrest the marchers. King was put inside a grim, narrow cell that had no windows and no bed. He was forbidden from contacting anyone.

When President Kennedy learned of the harsh conditions under which King was being held, he contacted the authorities in Birmingham and warned them that an inquiry was under way. Immediately, conditions for King improved. He received a mattress to sleep on, a blanket, and permission to shower and shave. Kennedy called

Martin and Coretta Scott King and their children; from left, Martin III (age 5), Dexter Scott (age 2), and Yolanda Denise (age 7)

Coretta King to assure her that "we've checked on your husband, and he's all right."[3] King's jailers then permitted him to take a call from his wife.

King had no writing paper in his cell, but he wanted to record his impressions. At first he wrote on margins of *The Birmingham News* daily newspaper and scraps of toilet paper. A black guard then passed him some bits of paper, and finally his lawyer gave him a note pad. King's writings from his jail cell became "Letter from Birmingham Jail," a powerful statement telling black people that they should not wait any longer for their rights. King wrote, "This 'Wait' has always meant 'Never.' We have waited for more than 340 years for our constitutional and God-given rights."[4] King's nine-thousand-word letter has become a classic in protest literature.

On April 20, King and those who had been arrested with him paid their bail and were released. On April 23, King was convicted, then released on bail again while he filed an appeal.

Another Birmingham demonstration, consisting largely of black children and teenagers, was planned. On May 2, the protest that would become known as the Children's Crusade got under way with nearly one thousand youngsters ranging in age from six to sixteen. A police officer confronted an eight-year-old and demanded to know what she wanted. "Freedom!" the little girl shouted.[5] All the young people were arrested. There was not enough room for them in the local jails, so they were held in outdoor pens in the hot sun without sanitary facilities. The Birmingham authorities hoped the unpleasant experience would discourage the children from further protests.

Another demonstration quickly followed. The group, which included children and adults, began shouting, "We want freedom."[6] A frustrated Bull Connor ordered his firemen to force the protestors to stop. After powerful German shepherds charged into the crowd, biting some of the marchers, high-pressure hoses were aimed at the protestors. The stream of water was so powerful that people were smashed against buildings and bark was stripped from trees. As children were swept down the street, some suffered broken arms and ribs. Connor's men then waded into the crowd, beating the protesters with fists, feet, and billy clubs.

Bull Connor ordered the Birmingham firemen to stop the protestors by any means necessary. "Let 'em have it," he said.[7]

President Kennedy watched the violence on television. He said the sight of children being attacked like that made him "sick."[7] Kennedy added that he could well understand the unwillingness of blacks to wait any longer for equality.

The outrage across the country was so great that Birmingham city officials finally agreed to negotiate with the African American community. King and his allies made four demands. First, complete desegregation of all facilities in the downtown stores; second, the hiring of blacks in sales and clerical positions; third, the institution of a permanent biracial committee to work on desegregating the whole city. The fourth and final demand was the release from jail of all the protestors.

When Birmingham officials agreed to the demands, King was overjoyed. But the results of the agreement

Birmingham police commissioner Bull Connor directs the arrests of African American protestors in April 1963.

were not all positive. Angry whites resented the advances blacks had made. Some resorted to violence. The front of A. D. King's home was blown away by a bomb. Still, the struggle in Birmingham had been a success, and it firmly established Martin Luther King Jr., as the national leader in the drive for black equality. It also raised the prestige of the SCLC as an organization that could be depended upon to produce results.

A Man in Demand

King had been thrust into national prominence by the Birmingham success, and he was now greatly in demand all over the country for speeches. He spoke to thousands of people in Chicago, Detroit, and Los Angeles. With the momentum so strong in favor of black equality,

Attorney General Robert Kennedy urged his brother to initiate major civil rights legislation. In June 1963, President Kennedy introduced sweeping legislation to outlaw segregation in interstate public accommodations throughout the country. The federal government would be authorized to force school integration and shut off aid to all programs that practiced discrimination.

The news caused joy for those in the civil rights movement and bitter resentment among white

WHO WAS MEDGAR EVERS?

Medgar Evers, Mississippi's best-known activist for civil rights, became a martyr to the struggle for equality in 1963. As field secretary of the NAACP in Mississippi, Evers motivated African Americans to register to vote, organized a boycott of stores in Jackson, Mississippi, and worked to end segregation. The enemies of civil rights hated Evers, and one of them murdered him. This first assassination of a black civil rights leader set off race riots as far away as Harlem, New York. Martin Luther King Jr., came to Evers's funeral and, as he always did, counseled nonviolence even in the face of murder.

segregationists who did not want anything to change. The day after Kennedy's announcement, Medgar Evers, an activist in the Mississippi NAACP, was shot to death in front of his house in Jackson, Mississippi. The state of Mississippi disregarded all integration efforts by the federal government, and civil rights marchers there were brutally beaten. On June 22, 1963, President Kennedy invited King and other civil rights leaders to the White House to address the problem.

A Risky March

Philip Randolph, who in 1925 had founded the largest black labor group in America, the Brotherhood of Sleeping Car Porters, came up with an idea at the White House meeting. He urged a large march on Washington, DC, made up of blacks and sympathetic whites, calling for immediate racial equality in America. President Kennedy did not like the idea, but King embraced it. Kennedy pleaded with King to abandon the plan, warning him that it might lead to bloodshed and a backlash against black people.

"Mr. President," King insisted, "the masses are restless, and we will march. We will have a march on Washington."[9] Kennedy continued to argue that the march would get out of control, ending in violence. He feared his civil rights legislation would be doomed. But King and the other black leaders would not be moved. They began to make plans for a summer march on Washington.

At this time, Martin Luther King Jr., was under investigation by J. Edgar Hoover, who headed the Federal Bureau of Investigation (FBI). For many years, Hoover had been convinced that the Communist Party in the United States was using the civil rights movement to recruit members and undermine the US government.

Ever since Russia had adopted a communist government in 1917, many people had feared that communism would take over the United States. Communism is a political philosophy that the government should own all property, which should then be distributed equally among the citizens of a country. After World War II, communism had spread to several countries, including Eastern Europe, China, and Cuba. Communist leaders hoped to spread their ideology worldwide, often by infiltrating groups and then starting a revolution. Officials like Hoover worried about the influence of communism in the United States. So the FBI kept an "enemies list" of people seen as threats to the American way of life.

Martin Luther King Jr. was on the list of America's most dangerous enemies. Although King was on record as denouncing communism as a fraud, Hoover ignored this fact. Hoover was determined to gather evidence against King that would prove him to be a communist agent. He asked Attorney General Robert Kennedy for permission to plant listening devices in King's offices and in hotels and motels where King stayed. Kennedy granted this request.

Unaware of the massive effort to discredit him as a communist agent, King issued a call for all blacks and whites friendly to the cause to make plans to come to Washington by car, train, bus, or plane. The march was scheduled for August 28, 1963, and the theme was "jobs and freedom."

Hoover hoped he could amass enough evidence against King before the march to destroy his credibility. He feared that a successful march would catapult King into such a powerful position that he could no longer be stopped.

6

"We Can't Wait"

August 28, 1963, was a typically hot and humid summer day in Washington, DC. That didn't stop thousands of people of all races and religions from gathering at the famous Lincoln Memorial. They had arrived on cars, trains, buses, bicycles, and even on foot to attend the jobs and freedom rally. The crowd heard speakers and musicians call for racial equality. But most had come to hear Dr. King's speech, not realizing that it would become one of the most celebrated in American history.

Here, King delivered his most famous words in what became known as the "I Have a Dream" speech. It was a passionate, eloquent call for the equality of all people. "I have a dream," King said in one of the most memorable lines, "that my four little children will one day live in a nation where they will not be judged by the color of their skin, but by the content of their character."[1] King concluded his speech with the hope that "all God's children, black men and white men, Jews and gentiles, Protestants and Catholics, will be able to join hands and sing in the words of that old Negro spiritual, 'Free at last! Free at last! Thank God Almighty, we are free at last!'"[2]

The stunning speech, delivered with great power and emotion, left the crowd shouting with joy. Many were weeping and crying out King's name. President Kennedy, who had worried so much about the march, was delighted by how smoothly everything went. He invited King and some of the other march organizers to the White House for lunch. It was a moment of triumph for King and the whole civil rights movement. All the other demonstrations had been leading to this day, and now it appeared that the nation was uniting in a desire to make the dream of equality a reality for all Americans.

But J. Edgar Hoover was unhappy at the attention King was getting. He had described King as "the most dangerous Negro of the future in this nation from the standpoint of Communism."[3] Now it seemed to Hoover that this dangerous man was making even more serious inroads to the heart of the nation. Hoover's agents had not stopped King before the march, but they did not give up.

Threat from the FBI

After the march, King and other civil rights leaders went to their suite in the Willard Hotel in Washington. Inside, everyone was in high spirits after the success of the day. The FBI knew King and his party would celebrate there

King waves to the crowd gathered at the Lincoln Memorial on
August 28, 1963, just prior to delivering his famous
"I Have a Dream" speech.

after the march, and the agents were ready. They had planted listening devices in the suite and were recording everything. After the party, the tapes were retrieved and sent to Hoover. He listened to them, then sent them on to Attorney General Kennedy. Robert Kennedy agreed to increase the spying on King, and electronic devices were planted in King's home phone and in all SCLC telephones to check for communist connections.

Attorney General Kennedy thought that if the tapes revealed no communist connections to King, then Hoover would give up his campaign against King. However, if any proof were uncovered, Kennedy planned to confront King with the evidence and demand that he cut off all contact with friends who were members of the Communist Party.

Meanwhile, Hoover was busy making copies of the Willard Hotel tapes, hoping these would undermine King. He sent copies to the White House, the secretary of state, the Defense Department, the CIA, and the Joint Chiefs of Staff. At the time, King had no idea that all this was happening.

On Sunday morning, September 15, 1963, one of the most horrendous acts of violence committed during the civil rights struggle took place. A bomb exploded in Birmingham's Sixteenth Street Baptist Church, a center for rallies and marches. Four young girls in the back of the church were putting on their choir robes, and all four died instantly. King was shocked and horrified by the "sin and evil" of this act.[4] He came as close to utter despair as he ever would. King was preaching at Ebenezer Baptist Church when the bombing took place, and he traveled immediately to Birmingham. At the funeral for the girls, King described them as "heroines of a holy crusade for freedom and human dignity."[5]

J. Edgar Hoover was the director of the Federal Bureau of Investigation (FBI) for forty-eight years. Hoover was one of King's biggest critics.

Personal Issues

King's personal life in 1963 was, by his own admission, "troubled."[6] King, who had been raised in comfort, sometimes felt guilty that he had not suffered as most of his black brothers and sisters had. He worried that he had not earned all the praise he received. King kept looking for ways to sacrifice himself for the cause in the hopes of being more deserving as a leader. He had a very strong conscience, and he lamented the times when he had fallen short of his high ideals. "I am conscious of two Martin Luther Kings," he said later, describing a constant battle against his "lower self."[7] His feelings of guilt and self-doubt brought on bouts of insomnia and stomach pains.

On November 22, 1963, King was working on his book and half listening to the radio. When he heard the shocking news that President John F. Kennedy had been assassinated, he said to his wife, "This is sick. You just can't do right and survive in this nation."[8] Deeply shaken and close to tears, King said, "This is going to happen to me too. I just realized it. It's true, Corrie. I'll never see my fortieth birthday."[9] Coretta King had no words of solace for her husband.

The news of John F. Kennedy's assassination shocked and saddened Martin Luther King Jr. He not only lost a friend and supporter, but he also realized the threats on his own life, too.

King attended the funeral of President Kennedy at St. Matthew's Cathedral in Washington, DC. The new

SCHWERNER, CHANEY AND GOODMAN

African American Mississippi native James Chaney and two young Jewish Americans from New York, Andrew Goodman and Michael "Mickey" Schwerner, spent June 1964 in Mississippi as part of the Freedom Summer campaign. Its purpose was to help register African Americans to vote. When they disappeared, foul play was immediately suspected, although their bodies were not discovered until August. In 1967, seven white men were found guilty of the crime. However, none served more than six years in prison. The case was reopened years later and, in 2005, a Klansman named Edgar Ray Killen was found guilty of manslaughter for directing the murders. He was sentenced to sixty years in prison.

president, Lyndon Johnson, vowed that in honor of the slain Kennedy, he would see that the civil rights bill was passed. King met with Johnson in December 1963. Although he respected the new president, he did not have the same relationship with him that he had had with Kennedy.

King now turned to the civil rights struggles going on in St. Augustine, Florida. During a protest march against a segregated hotel, he and his fellow marchers were arrested. King was roughly treated and shoved into a jail cell. He said of the experience, "I've been in fifteen jails, but this is the first time that I have been treated like a hog."[10] The St. Augustine campaign achieved only modest gains, but in Washington, the legislation known as the 1964 Civil Rights Act was passed and signed by President Johnson. The bill banned discrimination in jobs, voting, and all public accommodations.

As King well knew, passing a new civil rights act would not change people's hearts. Desegregation would not come easily to the Deep South. This was once again shown to be true in June 1964, when three young civil rights workers were stopped for a traffic violation. Andrew Goodman and Michael Schwerner were white. James Chaney was black. The three men were then arrested in Neshoba County, Mississippi. They were released and told to get out of the area. Some members of the Ku Klux Klan followed the trio, overtook their car, and drove them out to a lonely road.

When it was discovered that the three men were missing, it was immediately feared that they had met with foul play. A Klansman eventually told the FBI where to search, and their bodies were discovered. They had been beaten, shot, and buried under an earthen dam in the hopes that their graves might be overlooked. Saddened by the new atrocity, and exhausted from his heavy work schedule, King checked into a hospital. Coretta visited her husband there with some great news—he had been awarded the Nobel Peace Prize for 1964.

A Controversial Stand

The Nobel Peace Prize is one of the world's most revered honors. It is given to the person or people who most fostered the spirit of peace during the previous year. Winners of the Nobel Peace prize nearly always earn world respect. There are material rewards as well, including a prized gold medal, a certificate, a diploma, and money. In 1964, the cash prize was $54,000. King accepted the cash but kept none of it. He donated every cent to civil rights organizations: $12,000 to the SCLC, $17,000 to the Council for United Civil Rights Leadership, and the remaining $25,000 to a special fund that was part of the SCLC.[1]

Still recovering from exhaustion in St. Joseph's Hospital in Atlanta, King received a visit from the city's Catholic archbishop Paul Halliman. The archbishop congratulated King on receiving the Nobel Prize, and blessed him. Then, to King's surprise, Halliman dropped to his knees and asked King, "May I receive your blessing?" Humbled by the gesture, King obliged.[2]

King went to Oslo, Norway, in December 1964, to receive the Nobel Peace Prize in a moving ceremony. But his elation was not to last. J. Edgar Hoover, who had described King as "the most notorious liar in America," believed that he now had the evidence to discredit

Martin Luther King displays his Nobel Peace Prize medal in Oslo, Norway, on December 10, 1964.

King.[3] In January 1965, Coretta Scott King found an anonymous package mailed to her from Miami, Florida. Inside the package was a tape and a note addressed to King, which said in part, "King, like all frauds your end is approaching." Along with crude insults, the note also suggested that King had "but one way out," hinting that he should commit suicide.[4]

Coretta King called her husband, and they both read the note. It claimed the tape was a copy of the FBI recording of the party in the Willard Hotel. The FBI expected King to be embarrassed that his partying had been caught on tape, but he insisted that the tape be played to Coretta and some civil rights allies. Years later, commenting on the contents of the tape, Coretta King said, "We found much of it unintelligible. We concluded that there was nothing in the tape to discredit him."[5] However, the whole incident left King shaken and frightened. "They are out to break me," he said. "They are out to get me, harass me, break my spirit." A despondent King, unafraid to admit to his own shortcomings, insisted that whatever happened in his life was "between me and my God."[6] For a while King deliberated whether or not he should keep the public speaking commitments he had made. After some soul searching, he decided to go on as usual.

> "In the final analysis, God does not judge us by the separate incidents or the separate mistakes that we make, but by the total bent of our lives."[7]

Undaunted by the failure of the tape to ruin King, the FBI continued to watch him. Everywhere King went, there was electronic surveillance. His hotel and meeting rooms were all bugged. The bugging became a joke to King and his allies. Before every meeting, they would acknowledge the spying by greeting J. Edgar Hoover as if he were in the room: "How are you doing?"

Selma

A march for voting rights was scheduled to begin March 7, 1965, in Selma, Alabama, and end in Montgomery. King was not planning to be a part of the march, but he watched developments closely. Hundreds of demonstrators headed for the Edmund Pettus Bridge on their way to Montgomery where they were confronted by Alabama state troopers. When the marchers would not obey orders to turn around and return to Selma, the troopers on horseback charged into the crowd. They rode right over the marchers, knocking them down and beating them with clubs. The troopers, in gas masks, then released a stream of gas that left the marchers sick and gasping.

King is flanked by his friend Ralph David Abernathy (*on the left*) and diplomat Ralph Bunche (*on the right*) during the third Selma to Montgomery march on March 21, 1965.

All over America that night, television programming was interrupted to show the brutal violence. President Johnson looked at the gruesome photos of wounded marchers and denounced what had happened. King, guilt-ridden that he was not there with the beleaguered marchers, rushed to Alabama. On March 9, 1965, King helped lead another march toward Montgomery. The marchers were halted, but this time there was no violence.

President Johnson addressed a joint session of Congress on March 15, 1965, calling what had happened to the marchers "an American tragedy."[8] He asked for swift passage of the 1965 Voting Rights Act, which would eliminate all qualifying tests for voter registration. On August 5, the president signed the act into law. King was grateful for President Johnson's efforts to advance civil rights. However, another issue was about to drive a serious wedge between the two men.

At the end of 1965, thousands of American soldiers were fighting in a war in Vietnam. Casualties mounted as the United States tried to keep South Vietnam from becoming a communist nation like North Vietnam. Many Americans

The Vietnam War started slowly but by the mid-1960s had grown into
a bloody conflict that was dividing the country. In this photo,
American troops march near Bien Hua, Vietnam, in May 1965.

opposed the war, but President Johnson insisted that unless the communists were stopped in Vietnam, all Asia was in danger of falling to communism.

Martin Luther King Jr., believed the war was sapping the moral and economic energy of the United States. Americans were bombing Vietnam and enemy camps in surrounding countries, and there were many civilian casualties. After seeing magazine photos of severely burned Vietnamese children, King vowed to "do everything I can to end that war."[9] But he did not speak publicly against the war at that time. Instead, he turned his attention to poverty and racial injustice in Chicago.

After many years of fighting discrimination in the South, King now concerned himself with the plight of poor people in the slums of Chicago, whose lives were scarred by unemployment and poor housing. It was King's first campaign in the North.

To show his commitment, King moved his family into a run-down apartment in the tenement district of Chicago at the intersection of Sixteenth Street and Hamlin Avenue. When Coretta King first saw this grim part of the city, she lamented, "There's nothing green in sight."[10] It would be the first time King had ever lived like this. The house had two bedrooms, a kitchen, and bathroom. The gas stove did not work, and plaster was crumbling and falling.

King decided to focus on housing segregation, leading marchers into white neighborhoods in a nonviolent demand for change. Later, historians would generally conclude that King's Chicago Freedom Movement of 1966 was a failure that did not bring about reforms.

As the Vietnam War raged on, Martin Luther King Jr. made his first public antiwar speech on April 4, 1967. He called for an end to the bombing and for immediate

King calls for an end to racial injustice and poverty during the Chicago campaign in July 1966.

peace negotiations. "Somehow this madness must cease," he said. "We must stop now. I speak as a child of God and brother to the suffering poor of Vietnam."[11]

The Critics Speak Out

A firestorm of criticism followed. Respected magazines like *Newsweek* and *Life*, and newspapers including *The New York Times* and *The Washington Post*, all denounced King's remarks. Many of King's loyal friends—such as Whitney Young of the National Urban League, Roy Wilkins of the NAACP, sports icon Jackie Robinson, and African American senator Edward Brooke—

condemned King's position on the war. Even the SCLC asked King to be silent on the subject.

King's friend Andrew Young described the civil rights leader as being "almost reduced to tears," but "on fire with determination."[12] "I know I'm right," King told his wife. "I know this is an unjust and evil war."[13] King refused to retreat from his position and his public comments, admitting that it was "a low period in my life."[14] He insisted that the Vietnam War "practically destroyed Vietnam and left thousands of American and Vietnamese youth

NEW METHODS OF RESISTANCE

When Martin Luther King Jr. went to Chicago to fight for decent housing for the poor, he met angry young blacks who belonged to a rising new segment of the African American community. This militant group also called for equal rights, however some of its members rejected King's commitment to nonviolence. Groups like the Black Liberation Army, the Black Students Union, and the Black Panthers showed disdain for King's methods. They promoted riots and even armed rebellion. This added tension would lead to rifts within the civil rights movement over the most effective tactics that could be used for racial justice.

maimed and mutilated," adding that "we [must] end the nightmarish war and free our souls."[15]

In December 1967, Martin Luther King was planning an even larger campaign on behalf of poor people of all colors. He wanted to bring thousands of poor Americans to the Washington Monument, where they would put up a tent city to symbolize the lack of decent housing for the poor. President Johnson opposed the idea, and more criticism came King's way.

After a brief vacation in Jamaica and Mexico, the Kings returned to the United States to learn of yet another struggle he could aid in, a labor crisis in Memphis, Tennessee. Black sanitation workers needed his help. This would turn out to be King's last battle.

"We Are Tired"

On the morning of February 1, 1968, sanitation workers Robert Walker and Echol Cole hopped on board a garbage truck they would be riding through a pleasant east Memphis neighborhood for the next ten hours. Because garbage workers were considered unclassified laborers by the Memphis city government, their pay was pitiful and they had no benefits such as medical insurance. The weather that day was typical for a Memphis winter: cool and rainy. They spent that day in the rain emptying people's trash into their truck. When their rounds were finished, they headed for the dump.

By the late afternoon, the men's clothes were covered with the spillover of that day's trash. It included everything from rotten food to yard waste. Because of the constant rain showers, they were also soaking wet. They were messy and smelly and took a break from the weather by climbing into the covered back of the truck where the trash was kept before it was compacted. But the compactor mechanism malfunctioned. The compactor motor accidentally started and the men were crushed to death. The families of Walker and Cole suddenly had no money coming in. They went to the city government for help but the city officials told them there was nothing they could do.

Striking sanitation workers march in Memphis as National Guard soldiers keep watch.

On that same rainy day, black sewer workers were sent home without pay, but their white supervisors were kept on, with pay. These incidents triggered the Memphis sanitation workers to strike. The sanitation and sewer workers of Memphis received no worker's compensation to provide a temporary salary in case they were injured on the job, and no overtime pay when they worked more than eight hours a day. They were the lowest paid workers in the city. To improve their conditions, they formed a union to represent them in negotiations with Memphis authorities. The city refused to recognize their union.

The Memphis workers walked off the job and went on strike, carrying signs proclaiming, "I AM A MAN."[1] The city threatened to fire them all and bring in new workers to replace them. A local judge issued an injunction ordering all protest marchers to stop. The workers of Memphis were losing hope, and they did not know where to turn. Reverend James Lawson of Memphis, an old friend of Martin Luther King's, asked King to come to Memphis and lend his prestige and support to the cause.

The SCLC staff tried to discourage King from going to Memphis. He had a heavy schedule of speeches in Georgia, Alabama, and Mississippi. The Poor People's Campaign was getting started, and the march on Washington to build a tent city there would be a huge undertaking. King's aides insisted that he did not have time to go to Memphis. King responded, "These are poor folks. If we don't stop for them, then we don't need to go to Washington. These are part of the people we're going there for."[2]

To make time for the people in Memphis, King quickly crisscrossed the South, speaking to thousands of people. In just one day, he stopped in seven towns in Mississippi, making speeches in all of them. His energy was unbounded. Once he had fulfilled all his speaking engagements, he was free to help his friends in Memphis.

A Large Crowd Awaits

On March 18, King arrived in Memphis. He conferred with local leaders and then went to the Masonic Temple to make a speech. He expected to just give a short pep talk, but when he arrived, thousands of people awaited him.

King's speech was powerful and stirring. "We are tired of being at the bottom," he told the cheering crowd. "We are tired of working our hands off and laboring every day and not even making a wage adequate with the daily basic necessities of life."[3] As the theme of "we are tired," continued, the people were energized. Their feelings of hopelessness gave rise to a new enthusiasm. King had planned to make his short speech in Memphis and then get on with his schedule in other places. But he was so moved by the gratitude of the people that he decided to return to Memphis in ten days to personally lead the protest march on behalf of the striking workers.

The march was set for Thursday, March 28. King helped plan for the event. The black people of Memphis were encouraged to boycott their jobs that day. Black students were urged to stay out of school. The entire black community of Memphis was asked to support the sanitation workers.

Martin Luther King and Reverend Ralph Abernathy led the march, but disaster struck almost immediately. Some angry black youths smashed store windows along the march route. The police moved in with riot gear. King and Abernathy left the march. King explained, "I will never lead a violent march."[4]

King was brokenhearted about what had taken place. In the thirteen years that he had led nonviolent marches all across the South, nothing like this had ever happened. By the next day King had resolved the problem in his mind. He believed he could have talked the violent youths out of their actions if he had known ahead of time what they had planned. He promised to return to Memphis in a week and vowed that the next demonstration would be nonviolent.

On April 3, King arrived in Memphis in good spirits. President Johnson had announced that he would not run for reelection in 1968, and King hoped this would hasten the end of the Vietnam War. Though suffering from a sore throat, King went out in a rainstorm to speak to a crowd at the Masonic Temple. His reception was so loud that it blocked out the thunder of the storm outside.

A Moving Speech

At the Masonic Temple, Martin Luther King delivered one of the most moving and passionate speeches of his life. "I've Been to the Mountaintop," he said. He pleaded for a nonviolent march on April 5. He recalled the civil rights struggles of the past and told the crowd: "I've seen the promised land. I may not get there with you. But I want you to know tonight that we as a people will get to the promised land."[5]

On the morning of April 4, King met with his staff about the march set for the following day. The judge had lifted an injunction against the march, so it would be a legal protest. King's brother, A. D., was with him and they called their mother in Atlanta. King met with some black youths who had gang connections, and he pleaded with them to reject violence.

Two men hold replicas of the protest signs sanitation workers carried while on strike at the Lorraine Motel, site of King's assassination on April 4, 1968.

At 6:00 p.m. King and Abernathy were getting ready to leave their room at the Lorraine Motel and go out to dinner. King stepped out on the iron balcony to talk to some people in the courtyard below, including a musician he knew. "Ben," King called, "I want you to sing for me tonight. I want you to do that song 'Precious Lord.' Sing it real pretty."[6]

Seconds later, a bullet, apparently from the direction of a rooming house across the street, hit King in his lower right jaw. The single bullet smashed his jawbone, then pierced his neck, ripping open major blood vessels and nerves. It severed his spinal cord before lodging in his shoulder blade.

Ralph Abernathy was close by when King was struck. He recalled later, "I looked down at Martin's face. His eyes wobbled." Abernathy knelt beside his friend and said, "Martin, it's all right. Don't worry. This is Ralph. This is Ralph."[7] The force of the bullet had hurled King backward. He lay on the balcony floor, his feet sticking through the railing. Abernathy pressed a towel to the terrible wound in an effort to stop the rapid bleeding. The bullet had removed the right side of King's jaw and his head lay in a pool of blood. Abernathy and some others put a pillow under King's head as the frantic call for help went out.

When the ambulance arrived, paramedics rushed King to St. Joseph's Hospital. Abernathy rode in the ambulance and helped the paramedics check King's faint pulse and give him oxygen. King was taken to the emergency room at the hospital where a team of doctors and nurses cut the shirt and coat from his body and massaged his heart. The medical team worked frantically, but King could not be saved.

The neurosurgeon in charge of the effort to save King's life told Abernathy, "I'm afraid it's over." At 7:05 p.m., April 4, 1968, the head physician said, "I'm sorry, but we've lost him. It's all over."[8]

Abernathy collected King's belongings, including his wallet and checkbook. Then he and other friends who had gathered at the hospital hugged one another and left. Martin Luther King's parents in Atlanta heard the news of their son's death on the radio. Daddy King later remembered the horror of that moment: "My first son, whose birth had brought me such joy that I jumped up in the hall outside the room where he was born and touched the ceiling—the child, the scholar, the preacher ... all of it was gone."[9]

Coretta King had just returned from a shopping trip with her children when she received a phone call from family friend Jesse Jackson. He told her that her husband had been shot and that she should come to Memphis as quickly as possible. He did not tell her that King was dead. The Kings' eldest child, Yolanda, was watching television when the news bulletin came on, announcing her father's death. The girl screamed. Coretta King rushed to the Atlanta airport to take a flight to Memphis. When she reached the airport, she was escorted into a private room, where the mayor of Atlanta was waiting for her. He told her that her husband had died of the wounds he suffered. Coretta King now had no reason to hurry. She had four children at home who needed her desperately. She returned to the family home, where she found Yolanda praying behind the living room curtain, "Lord, please take care of my mommy and make her strong."[10] Coretta comforted her daughter. She told the child not

King's casket is carried on a caisson pulled by mules during his funeral procession in Atlanta.

to hate the person who killed her father. Yolanda told herself, "My daddy's not really dead, and I'm going to see him again in heaven."[11]

On Dr. Martin Luther King Jr.'s tombstone is written: "Free at last, free at last, thank God Almighty I'm free at last."[12]

Coretta King and her three older children went to Memphis on April 8 to take part in a memorial march honoring the part King had played in the resolution of the Memphis sanitation workers strike. All the demands of the workers had been quickly agreed to by the city of Memphis.

King's body was returned to Atlanta, where he lay in state in Sisters Chapel at Spelman College. Mourners came by the thousands. Each hour about twelve hundred people filed past the casket, pausing to honor the great leader. On April 9, eight hundred people gathered inside Ebenezer Baptist Church for the funeral service. A hundred thousand more heard the proceedings outside on loudspeakers.[13] All the famous civil rights leaders of the day, along with numerous celebrities, attended. Former attorney general Robert Kennedy and future president Richard Nixon joined Vice President Hubert Humphrey. Jacqueline Kennedy, widow of the assassinated president John F. Kennedy, mourned alongside King's many close friends.

The choir sang many of King's favorite hymns. Coretta King asked that the recording of a sermon King had given at Ebenezer Church in February, titled "A Drum Major

THE KING CENTER

A year after King's death, Coretta King announced her intention to develop the Martin Luther King Jr. Center for Nonviolent Social Change in Atlanta. She devoted most of her time and energy in the following months and years to making this center a reality. The goal of the center was to promote Martin Luther King's values. Gifts, large and small, poured into Atlanta for the center, and in 1979, construction began. In January 1982, the center was officially opened. There was a church, an exhibition center, meeting rooms, and a reflecting pool. King's body was brought from South View Cemetery and placed in an elevated marble crypt at the Freedom Hall complex in the center.

for Justice," be played at the funeral. In the sermon, King had responded to the question, "What would you like to be said on the day of your funeral?" He said, "Say that I was a drum major for peace. I was a drum major for righteousness."[14] When the Kings' youngest child, five-year-old Bernice, heard her father's voice, she turned her head around, searching for him.

Thousands walked in slow procession behind the special vehicle, called a poor person's hearse. It was a farm cart drawn by two mules. It carried King's body to South View Cemetery. The cemetery was blooming with dogwoods and fresh green boughs as King was laid to rest near the grave of his beloved grandmother Williams. On his tomb were the words "Free at last, free at last, thank God Almighty I'm free at last."[15]

The Years Since

In the wake of King's murder, President Lyndon Johnson announced to the nation, "I ask every American citizen to reject the blind violence that has struck Dr. King who lived by non-violence."[1] But it was not to be. Outraged African Americans took their anger out by gathering in city streets across the country. The result was chaos and rioting. Mobs damaged buildings and set fires in many cities. One of the hardest hit was Washington, DC, where federal troops patrolled the city for the first time since the Civil War. To many rioters, Dr. King's dream had gone up in smoke.

The investigation into King's death began immediately, but it would be two months before the assassin was caught. An ex-convict named James Earl Ray was an early suspect after police found a bundle on the sidewalk near the Lorraine Motel. Inside was a Remington 30.06 Gamemaster rifle with a spent cartridge and ammunition. It belonged to Ray, whose fingerprints were on the rifle.

Ray had been born in 1928 in Illinois. He was from a poor, working-class family. He learned to dislike African Americans from his father, who blamed them for many of society's problems. Ray also learned bigotry from the frustrated poor whites in his neighborhood, who were looking for somebody to blame for their plight. As a

The tombs of Martin and Coretta Scott King are in the plaza on the grounds of the Martin Luther King Jr. Center for Non-Violent Social Change, a short walk from where King was born.

child, Ray was a loner, frequently tormented by his peers for his dirty, ragged clothing and shyness. One of his teachers, writing an evaluation of the boy, described him as "repulsive."[2]

> **James Earl Ray learned bigotry from his father and from the frustrated poor whites in his neighborhood, who were looking for someone to blame for their plight.**

First arrested for stealing at age fourteen, Ray was constantly in trouble for burglaries and armed robberies. During his many stays in prison, he allied with the white

WANTED BY THE FBI

CIVIL RIGHTS - CONSPIRACY
INTERSTATE FLIGHT - ROBBERY
JAMES EARL RAY

FBI No. 405,942 G

Photographs taken 1960

Photograph taken 1968
(eyes drawn by artist)

Aliases: Eric Starvo Galt, W. C. Herron, Harvey Lowmyer, James McBride, James O'Conner, James Walton, James Walyon, John Willard, "Jim,"

DESCRIPTION

Age:	40, born March 10, 1928, at Quincy or Alton, Illinois (not supported by birth records)		
Height:	5' 10"	**Eyes:**	Blue
Weight:	163 to 174 pounds	**Complexion:**	Medium
Build:	Medium	**Race:**	White
Hair:	Brown, possibly cut short	**Nationality:**	American

Wanted posters like this one were distributed in the wake of King's assassination as authorities searched for assassin James Earl Ray.

convicts against the blacks. He refused to participate in prison sports if African Americans were involved. He admired German dictator Adolf Hitler because he believed Hitler would make the United States an "all white country, no Jews or Negroes."[3] He dreamed of moving to the British-ruled colony of Rhodesia in Africa, where the black majority was strictly segregated from the ruling whites. Ray's entire life was one of bitterness, rejection, and failure. He confided in an acquaintance that he longed to be important enough someday to be on the FBI's Most Wanted list.

Fifteen days after King's death, the FBI issued an all points bulletin for Ray. The evidence indicated that on April 4 he had positioned himself in the window of a rooming house across from the Lorraine Motel, aiming at King. With the help of the seven-times magnification on the rifle's scope, King appeared close. Ray was able to place the crosshairs of the rifle's scope in the middle of King's head before he pulled the trigger. Then, when he saw King fall, he rushed to his Ford Mustang and drove off.

He fled first to Canada, then to London, England, where he was arrested in June 1968. At his trial in March 1969, Ray plead guilty to shooting Martin Luther King Jr. and was sentenced to ninety-nine years in prison. Three days later, he withdrew his guilty plea, saying he had been forced to take the blame for the murder. For the next thirty years, until his death in prison in 1994, he claimed he was innocent of the crime. King's son, Dexter Scott King, was among those who believed in Ray's innocence. Conspiracy theories have been raised concerning the assassination of King, with accusations that the US government was involved. However, most experts believe that such a large government plot would have since been discovered by investigative journalists. But if Ray didn't act alone, perhaps some racists paid him to shoot King.

One week after the death of Martin Luther King Jr., the 1968 Civil Rights Act was passed. Called the Open Housing Act, it forbade any kind of housing discrimination in the United States. President Johnson immediately signed it into law.

The King Family

Coretta King had four young children to raise alone, so the 1970s were very challenging for her. But she found time to campaign to make her husband's birthday a national holiday in America. This was finally accomplished in 1986, when President Ronald Reagan signed it into law. During the 1970s, violent tragedy again struck the King family. Alberta King—Martin Luther King, Jr.'s mother—was playing the Lord's Prayer on the organ at Ebenezer Baptist Church in Atlanta on June 30, 1974, when a crazed man stood up in the congregation. He shot Alberta King to death, killed a deacon, and wounded another parishioner. The assassin, Marcus Wayne Chenault, was eventually sentenced to life in prison without parole.

In November 1984, Daddy King, the beloved pastor of Ebenezer Baptist Church from 1931 to 1975, and father of Martin Luther King, Jr., died of a heart attack at age eighty-four. In spite of the terrible toll violence had taken on him with the murders of his beloved son and wife, Daddy King had always refused to be overtaken by hatred.

At the culmination of the 1963 March on Washington for Jobs and Freedom, in the most memorable and stirring speech of his life, Dr. Martin Luther King Jr. expressed his hopes for his own four little children. His death deprived those children of their father when the eldest, Yolanda, was twelve, and the youngest, Bernice, was five. But in the shadow of their father's towering legacy and with their mother's guidance, the four children grew into successful adults.

SEPARATING MAN FROM MYTH

Reflecting on her father in 2004, Yolanda King said that when she sees pictures of him on television she feels awe, but the solemn man giving powerful sermons is not the father she remembers. She recalls instead the daddy who was "full of love and laughter." She thinks of him in the kitchen, dipping into the pots her mother was cooking with. Yolanda's mother would say, "Stop, Martin. You're setting a bad example for the kids." But when her back was turned, he would go right back to dipping.[4]

Tributes Pour In

In the aftermath of Martin Luther King Jr.'s death, there were hundreds of tributes. Cities across America named streets, schools, and public buildings in his honor. His legacy has been widespread. By exposing injustices against African Americans, he led the way for other minorities to begin campaigning in their own interests. His courageous work inspired many members of the clergy to become advocates of the poor and marginalized.

Barack Obama is sworn in as the forty-fourth—and first
African American—president of the United States on January 20,
2009. Obama's wife, Michelle, stands beside him.

Because of the civil rights movement, African Americans in the South gained equal access to public services and facilities. Before King started his marches, African Americans sat in the backs of buses and theaters, could not receive service in restaurants, and were often denied access to housing and good jobs. Their children attended inferior schools, and they were often denied the right to vote. But after King, a new vision of equality—although not always perfect—was realized.

CONCLUSION

On November 4, 2008, what would have seemed impossible just fifteen years earlier happened. Barack Obama was elected president of the United States. The notion of an African American US president seemed unreal to millions not only in America but across the world. In fact, when Obama officially received the nomination of the Democratic Party a few months earlier, many Democrats were disappointed. They liked Obama's views and they believed he would be a good president. But they thought the United States still wasn't ready to have a president who wasn't white. The fact that the president had a Muslim-sounding name made them feel even less optimistic. But, to the surprise of many people around the world, Obama won in a landslide.

The news of an African American president made banner headlines across the world. The headline of the United States's national newspaper, *USA Today*, shouted in large, bold type, "A dream fulfilled."[1] *USA Today* staff writer Rick Hampson wrote, "The day was a long time coming, and when Wednesday finally dawned, a lot of bleary-eyed, partied-out Americans had to pinch themselves: They had an African-American president-elect."[2]

A retired Memphis sanitation worker named Taylor Rogers, who had heard King speak the night before he was assassinated, said, "This was Dr. King's dream—to have someone in the black community to represent us, and bring the races together."[3]

Of course, as with any election, not everybody was happy. Disappointed voters and some conservative media began spreading false rumors about Obama. One was that he was born in Kenya, not the United States. Therefore,

The activist group Black Lives Matter was founded in 2014 as a result of multiple controversial police shootings of African American men.

he wouldn't be eligible to be president. Another was that he is secretly a Muslim. There are always sore losers after any election, so it is hard to tell how much of the rumor mongering was racist in intent. Then again, some Americans spewed out obvious racist hatred, leaving no doubt as to where they stood.

King's work to bring down white supremacy in the South was a great victory for human freedom. Yet prejudices continue to exist some sixty years later. In 2014, the news was dominated by reports of police killings of African Americans. This became a very touchy subject in the United States. African Americans and their allies believed black people were unfairly singled out by the police. They thought police were too quick to shoot—and in many cases kill—black suspects. In other cases, African Americans died while in police custody. In many, but not all the cases, the police officers involved were white.

Others thought the police were being unfairly criticized. Police work is a dangerous job. Police often have to make snap decisions whether or not to use violence when dealing with a suspect. There are many cases where their choices are to shoot or be shot.

In response, an activist group called Black Lives Matter (BLM) was founded. Its stated purpose is to protest against police brutality and racial profiling. BLM leaders urge non-violence. However, a few riots have broken out at BLM rallies, which hurt the group's image. Many have compared the BLM movement with Martin Luther King's work to guarantee equal rights for all Americans during the civil rights movement.

King used his mastery of the spoken word to arouse African Americans to march behind his banner of nonviolent protest. He allowed himself to be jailed twenty-nine times, to be beaten, spat on, humiliated, and ridiculed. Had he resorted to violence in his crusade for equality for black people, America could have been plunged into a horrifying race war. By appealing to the best in people, he led a peaceful revolution that changed America for the better.

Martin Luther King Jr. spoke of the triple evils of racism, poverty, and war. He showed how these could be constantly confronted, but he did not conquer any of them. The struggle against these evils continues, and it remains for all Americans to carry the banner he once did.

CHRONOLOGY

1929 Martin Luther King Jr. is born in Atlanta, Georgia on January 15.

1944 King skips his final year of high school to attend Morehouse College in Atlanta.

1948 King graduates from Morehouse College with a bachelor's degree in sociology and becomes associate pastor at Ebenezer Baptist Church in Atlanta, Georgia.

1951 King graduates from Crozer Theological Seminary in Chester, Pennsylvania, with a bachelor of divinity degree.

1953 King marries Coretta Scott on June 18.

1954 King becomes pastor of Dexter Avenue Baptist Church in Montgomery, Alabama.

1955 He receives a doctorate in divinity from Boston University; the Kings' first child, Yolanda Denise, is born in November; King becomes president of Montgomery Improvement Association (MIA) and leads a boycott of the segregated city bus system.

1957 King founds and becomes president of the Southern Christian Leadership Conference (SCLC); the family's second child, Martin Luther King III, is born in October; King receives the prestigious Spingarn Medal.

1958 His first book, *Stride Toward Freedom: The Montgomery Story*, is published; King is stabbed in Harlem by deranged woman.

1959 King and his wife visit India; King learns more about Gandhi techniques of nonviolence.

1960 The family moves to Atlanta, where King becomes co-pastor, with his father, of Ebenezer Baptist Church; he supports formation of the Student Nonviolent Coordinating Committee (SNCC), an organization for student protests and meets with President Kennedy about racial issues; King is arrested on charges of violating probation over a traffic charge.

1961 The family's third child, Dexter, is born in January; King supports the Freedom Riders and leads a march of segregation protesters in the Albany Movement.

1963 The family's fourth child, Bernice Albertine, is born in March; King's second book, *Strength to Love*, is published; he is arrested at demonstration against segregated lunch counters; "Letter from Birmingham Jail" is written from King's prison cell and he delivers his "I Have a Dream" speech in Washington, DC.

1964 King's book *Why We Can't Wait* is published; he is awarded the Nobel Peace Prize.

1965 King leads demonstrators for voting rights on a march from Selma to Montgomery, Alabama.

1966 King moves his family to a rented apartment in the poor section of Chicago to launch a campaign for better housing.

1967 King publicly opposes the Vietnam War; he writes the book *Where Do We Go From Here:*

Chaos or Community?; and he helps plan the Memphis March on behalf of striking sanitation and sewer workers.

1968 King delivers his last speech, "I've Been to the Mountaintop," in Memphis, Tennessee; he is assassinated in Memphis on April 4.

1986 King's birthday is first celebrated as a federal holiday.

2008 Barack Obama is elected as the first African American president of the United States, fulfilling a promise for greater racial equality that King fought for.

2011 The Martin Luther King Jr. Memorial opens on August 22, in Washington, DC.

CHAPTER NOTES

Introduction

1. Stephen S. Oates, *Let the Trumpet Sound: The Life of Martin Luther King, Jr.* (New York: Harper and Row, 1982), p. 134.

2. Ibid.

3. William Roger Witherspoon, *Martin Luther King: To the Mountaintop* (New York: Doubleday, 1985), p. 60.

4. Ibid.

5. Oates, p. 136.

Chapter 1: Life with Mother Dear and Daddy

1. Stephen S. Oates, *Let the Trumpet Sound: The Life of Martin Luther King, Jr.* (New York: Harper and Row, 1982), p. 5.

2. David J. Garrow, *Bearing the Cross: Martin Luther King, Jr., and the Southern Christian Leadership Conference* (New York: William Morrow, 1986), p. 33.

3. Adam Fairclough, *Martin Luther King, Jr.* (Athens, Georgia: University of Georgia Press, 1995), p. 6.

4. Clayborne Carson, ed., *The Autobiography of Martin Luther King, Jr.* (New York: Warner Books, 1998), p. 4.

5. Garrow, p. 34.

6. Martin Luther King, Jr., *Stride Toward Freedom: The Montgomery Story* (New York: Harper and Brothers, 1958), p. 20.

7. Stephen B. Oates, *Let the Trumpet Sound: The Life of Martin Luther King, Jr.* (New York: Harper and Row, 1982), pp. 9–10.

8. Garrow, p. 33.

9. Garrow, p. 38.

10. King, p. 19.

11. Carson, p. 7.

12. Garrow, p. 35.

13. Oates, p. 17.

14. Carson, p. 11.

Chapter 2: When Martin Met Coretta

1. William Roger Witherspoon, *Martin Luther King: To the Mountaintop* (New York: Doubleday, 1985), p. 5.

2. Stephen B. Oates, *Let the Trumpet Sound: The Life of Martin Luther King, Jr.* (New York: Harper and Row, 1982), p. 20.

3. Witherspoon, p. 8.

4. Ibid.

5. Witherspoon, pp. 10–11.

6. Clayborne Carson, ed., *The Autobiography of Martin Luther King, Jr.* (New York: Warner Books, 1998), p. 31.

7. Clayborne, p. 34.

8. Oates, p. 42.

9. Oates, p. 43.

10. Garrow, p. 45.

11. Oates, p. 43.

12. Witherspoon, p. 13.

13. Oates, p. 51.

Chapter 3: The Bus Was Empty!

1. Clayborne Carson, ed., *The Autobiography of Martin Luther King, Jr.* (New York: Warner Books, 1998), p. 49.

2. Martin Luther King, Jr., *Stride Toward Freedom: The Montgomery Story* (New York: Harper and Brothers, 1958), p. 53.

3. King, p. 63.

4. Adam Fairclough, *Martin Luther King, Jr.* (Athens, Georgia: University of Georgia Press, 1995), p. 24.

5. Fairclough, p. 48.

6. William Roger Witherspoon, *Martin Luther King: To the Mountaintop* (New York: Doubleday, 1985), p. 36.

7. King, pp. 134–135.

8. King, p. 137.

9. Witherspoon, p. 43.

10. King, p. 173.

11. Witherspoon, p. 52.

12. Witherspoon, p. 53.

13. Stephen B. Oates, *Let the Trumpet Sound: The Life of Martin Luther King*, Jr. (New York: Harper and Row, 1982), p. 138.

14. Charles Johnson and Bob Adelman, King: *The Autobiography of Martin Luther King, Jr.* (New York: Viking, 2000), p. 55.

15. Ibid.

16. Witherspoon, p. 61.

17. Oates, p. 143.

18. Oates, p. 146.

Chapter 4: The Jury Chose the "Path of Justice"

1. Stephen B. Oates, *Let the Trumpet Sound: The Life of Martin Luther King, Jr.* (New York: Harper and Row, 1982), p. 152.

2. William Roger Witherspoon, *Martin Luther King: To the Mountaintop* (New York: Doubleday, 1985), p. 71.

3. Oates, p. 152.

4. Oates, p. 155.

5. Oates, p. 156.

6. Witherspoon, p. 74.

7. Oates, p. 163.

8. Adam Fairclough, *Martin Luther King, Jr.* (Athens, Georgia: University of Georgia Press, 1996), p. 67.

9. Witherspoon, p. 107.

Chapter 5: Up Against Bull Connor

1. Donald T. Phillips, *Martin Luther King, Jr., on Leadership* (New York: Warner Books, 1999), p. 155.

2. Adam Fairclough, *Martin Luther King, Jr.* (Athens, Georgia: University of Georgia Press, 1995), p. 77

3. Ibid.

4. William Roger Witherspoon, *Martin Luther King: To the Mountaintop* (New York: Doubleday, 1985), p. 121.

5. Martin Luther King, Jr., *The Words of Martin Luther King, Jr.* (New York: Pocket Books, 1983), p. 38.

6. Phillips, p. 169.

7. Phillips, p. 170.

Chapter 6: "We Can't Wait"

1. Martin Luther King, Jr., *The Words of Martin Luther King, Jr.* (New York: Pocket Books, 1983), p. 83.

2. King, pp. 85–86.

3. William Roger Witherspoon, *Martin Luther King: To the Mountaintop* (New York: Doubleday, 1985), p. 144.

4. Stephen B. Oates, Let *the Trumpet Sound: The Life of Martin Luther King, Jr.* (New York: Harper and Row, 1982), p. 267.

5. Witherspoon, p. 149.

6. Oates, p. 281.

7. Oates, p. 283.

8. Witherspoon, p. 150.

9. Phillips, p. 310.

10. Donald T. Phillips, *Martin Luther King, Jr., on Leadership* (New York: Warner Books, 1999), p. 181.

Chapter 7: A Controversial Stand

1. William Roger Witherspoon, *Martin Luther King: To the Mountaintop* (New York: Doubleday, 1985), p. 167.

2. Ibid.

3. Adam Fairclough, *Martin Luther King, Jr.* (Athens, Georgia: University of Georgia Press, 1995), p. 99.

4. David J. Garrow, *Bearing the Cross: Martin Luther King, Jr., and the Southern Christian Leadership Conference* (New York: William Morrow, 1986), p. 373.

5. Stephen B. Oates, *Let the Trumpet Sound: The Life of Martin Luther King, Jr.* (New York: Harper and Row, 1982), p. 332.

6. Garrow, p. 374.

7. Oates, p. 333.

8. Witherspoon, p. 181.

9. Garrow, p. 543.

10. Charles Johnson and Bob Adelman, *King: The Autobiography of Martin Luther King, Jr.* (New York: Viking, 2000), p. 234.

11. Donald T. Phillips, Martin *Luther King, Jr., on Leadership* (New York: Warner Books, 1999), p. 294.

12. Witherspoon, p. 210.

13. Clayborne Carson, ed., *The Autobiography of Martin Luther King, Jr.* (New York: Warner Books, 1998), p. 342.

14. Carson, p. 345.

Chapter 8: "We Are Tired"

1. Gerald Posner, *Killing the Dream: James Earl Ray and the Assassination of Martin Luther King, Jr.* (New York: Random House, 1998), p. 3.

2. Donald T. Phillips, *Martin Luther King, Jr., on Leadership* (New York: Warner Books, 1999), pp. 322–323.

3. Phillips, p. 323.

4. Ibid.

5. Martin Luther King, Jr., *The Words of Martin Luther King, Jr.* (New York: Pocket Books, 1983), p. 80.

6. Posner, p. 30.

7. Ibid.

8. Stephen B. Oates, *Let the Trumpet Sound: The Life of Martin Luther King, Jr.* (New York: Harper and Row, 1982), p. 491.

9. Oates, p. 493.

10. William Roger Witherspoon, *Martin Luther King: To the Mountaintop* (New York: Doubleday, 1985), p. 223.

11. Ibid.

12. Witherspoon, p. 225.

13. Associated Press, *The Los Angeles Times*, April 5, 1968, p. 1.

14. Charles Johnson and Bob Adelman, *King: Autobiography of Martin Luther King, Jr.* (New York: Viking, 2000), p. 285.

15. Witherspoon, p. 225.

Chapter 9: The Years Since

1. Associated Press, "Johnson Saddened, Delays Hawaii Trip," *The Hartford Courant*, April 5, 1968, p. 1.

2. Gerald Posner, *Killing the Dream: James Earl Ray and the Assassination of Martin Luther King, Jr.* (New York: Random House, 1998), p. 332.

3. Posner, p. 83.

4. Karen M. Thomas, "Martin Luther King's Eldest Daughter Finds Her Own Way," *The San Diego Union*, April 22, 2004, p. E3.

Conclusion

1. *USA Today*, November 6, 2008, p. 1.

2. Rick Hampson, "For Many, A Sense That a New Era is Here," *USA Today*, November 6, 2008, p. 1.

3. Ibid.

GLOSSARY

boycott The refusal to buy a product or use a service, usually for a political reason.

colonialism The controlling of a nation or people by an unrelated government.

communism An economic and political system in which the government owns property and then distributes it equally to its citizens.

hymn A religious song with the purpose of praising a higher power.

integration The act of giving equal opportunities to people of all races and religions, especially regarding housing, jobs, education, and other basic human rights.

martial law An order enforced by a military or paramilitary group in times of civic unrest.

militant Aggressive and possibly violent behavior in support of a political cause.

probation The act of allowing a person guilty of a crime to be set free, but kept under the supervision of a law enforcement official.

scholarship Money or other form of material aid given to needy and intelligent students.

segregation The act of separating a minority group from the majority.

sharecropping Renting land from a landowner in order to farm it, in exchange for providing the landowner with a percentage of the crops farmed there.

sociology The study of human behavior as people interact with each other.

strike The act of refusing to work with the hopes that business owners will provide workers with better wages or better working conditions.

theology The study of religious beliefs.

union An organization of workers formed to insure themselves of fair wages and decent working conditions.

FURTHER READING

Books

Aretha, David. *Martin Luther King, Jr. and the 1963 March on Washington*. Greensboro, NC: Morgan Reynolds, 2014.

Bausum, Ann. *Marching to the Mountaintop*. Washington, DC: National Geographic Children's Books, 2012.

Boshier, Rosa. *How to Analyze the Works of Martin Luther King, Jr.,* Edina, MN: Abdo, 2013.

King, Martin Luther, Jr. *A Time to Break Silence: The Essential Works of Martin Luther King, Jr. for Students*. Boston, MA: Beacon Press, 2013.

Teitelbaum, Michael, and Lewis Helfand. *Martin Luther King, Jr.: Let Freedom Ring*. Hanover, NH: Campfire, 2013.

Websites

The King Center Archives
thekingcenter.org/archive
This King Center website offers digital copies of Martin Luther King Jr.'s sermons, speeches, and letters as well as articles about King and oral histories from people who knew him.

Martin Luther King Jr.: An Extraordinary Life
projects.seattletimes.com/mlk/bio.html#life
This website from *The Seattle Times* provides historic
    photo galleries, excerpts of famous speeches, and a
    biography of the famous civil rights leader.

The National Park Service: Martin Luther King Jr.
nps.gov/malu
The National Park Service website offers information
    about King's birthplace including a virtual tour, and
    information about the Sweet Auburn neighborhood.

INDEX